A BLACK
WAY OF
SEEING

A BLACK WAY OF SEEING

FROM "LIBERTY" TO FREEDOM

PAUL ROBESON, JR.

SEVEN STORIES PRESS
New York | Toronto | London | Melbourne

Seven Stories Press
140 Watts Street
New York, NY 10013
www.sevenstories.com/

In Canada
Publishers Group Canada, 559 College Street, Toronto, ON M6G 1A9

In the UK
Turnaround Publisher Services Ltd., Unit 3, Olympia Trading Estate,
Coburg Road, Wood Green, London N22 6TZ

In Australia
Palgrave Macmillan, 15–19 Claremont Street, South Yarra, VIC 3141

College professors may order examination copies of Seven Stories Press titles for a free six-month trial period. To order, visit www.sevenstories.com/textbook/ or send a fax on school letterhead to 212.226.1411.

Book design by Jon Gilbert

Library of Congress Cataloging-in-Publication Data

Robeson, Paul.
A Black way of seeing : from "liberty" to freedom / by Paul Robeson, Jr.—1st ed.
    p. cm.
  Includes bibliographical references and index.
  ISBN: 978-1-58322-767-1 (pbk. : alk. paper) / ISBN: 978-1-58322-725-1 (cl. : alk. paper)
  1. African Americans—Politics and government—20th century. 2. African Americans—Politics and government—21st century. 3. United States—Politics and government—20th century. 4. United States—Politics and government—2001–   5. African Americans—Race identity. 6. Black power—United States. 7. United States—Race relations. I. Title.
E185.615R523 2006
973'.0496076--dc22   2005036506

Printed in the USA

9 8 7 6 5 4 3 2 1

For my intrepid and courageous brothers and sisters from the low-lying wards of New Orleans who are determined to rebuild their city.

■ ■ ■

Many thanks to publisher Dan Simon for his patient discussion of the ideas behind this book and his suggestion of the title.

I am deeply grateful to my wife Marilyn for her creative and dedicated review of my manuscript, as well as for her penetrating questions about my underlying premises.

CONTENTS

INTRODUCTION

A Black Way of Seeing

1

CHAPTER I

9/11 In Black and White

21

CHAPTER II

Eight Coups in American History

31

CHAPTER III

The "War on Terror"

53

CHAPTER IV

Economics, Race, and Class

69

CHAPTER V

Class Commands

83

CHAPTER VI

Vote Fraud in 2000 and 2004

99

CHAPTER VII

Awaiting the Fifth Revolution

113

CHAPTER VIII
Black Destiny
153

APPENDIX A
The Anatomy of Two Vote Frauds
187

APPENDIX B
The Anatomy of the Switching Operation
195

Index
207

A BLACK WAY OF SEEING

I am a *free Black American.* I have a distinct culture. It derives from the traditional culture of African field slaves in the South. I identify with that culture by capitalizing the "B" in Black.

Some people say, "Why make so much of a name? It's divisive in these times, when we need to bring everyone together."

I reply, "We can come together only if we say who we really are. We must stop pretending that in the United States of America being Black or being white is the same."

Knowing who I am and what culture I come from is my foundation for leading a full and productive life. My roots in my own culture provide the doors and windows through which I communicate comfortably and constructively with people of other cultures. I also believe that it is time to end the virtual ban on public discussion of the differences between self-identification labels popularly used by various ethnic groups and within those groups. The labels need to be thoroughly aired out as part of a concerted effort to begin a nationwide public dialog on the twin topics of ethnicity and race. Despite misgivings in many quarters, such a discussion offers great benefit to our sorely divided nation in the long run.

My way of seeing is only one of millions of different Black ways of seeing, for there are as many such ways as there are Black people. However, all of these outlooks are similar in the sense that they are connected in varying degrees by the threads of a common culture that leads a majority of us to feel a special kinship for each other. Consequently, we have a tendency to act together in our common interest while seeing, feeling, and thinking independently.

Throughout this book, I speak only out of my own personal way of seeing, feeling, and thinking.

■ ■ ■

I chose my identification from a variety of commonly used terms: "black American," "Black American," "African-American," "African American." I chose "Black American" for several reasons. To me, "Black" means far more than a skin color, which is only a form of visual identification. Skin color varies over a vast range, from pale white to blue-black. It does not in any sense reflect human traits or human values, serving only as a crude and often mistaken indication of a person's continent of origin (Africa, Europe, Asia, the Americas, and so forth). However, by capitalizing the first letter of the color black I attach my culture to the color—the traditional culture of the field slaves from whom I am descended.

I say field slaves in order to make a distinction between field slaves and the small minority of privileged house slaves and skilled slaves (blacksmiths, teamsters, stone masons, horse breeders, planters, accountants, medical assistants, legal clerks) who enjoyed elite status in a complex slave hierarchy based on color and occupation. House slaves, who were placed at the top of the hierarchy, were generally lighter in skin color and more docile in personality than field slaves. They tended to identify with the master and his culture. The skilled slaves were assigned intermediate status on the basis of their valued skills, regardless of their color or personality. The field-slave majority constituted the bottom layer and rarely experienced direct contact with its master or with nonslave culture.

For this reason, the field slaves and the skilled slaves, who, unlike the house slaves, lived a good distance away from the grounds of the master's Big House, had considerable freedom to develop and maintain their own distinct common culture. They also were predominantly dark in skin color and remained so, since the lighter-skinned field slaves could rise into service in the Big House. They were also the driving force behind every slave rebellion. Malcolm X was referring to this history when he invoked the difference between the house slave and the field slave.

My personal choice of identification stems from my ancestry—my paternal grandfather was an escaped field slave. The term *black* without an upper-case *b* merely denotes a color and conveys no implicit identification with my field-slave cultural tradition. Therefore, it is unsatisfactory.

Finally, as a Black *American*, I assert my American identification as fully equal to that of any other American.

The term "African-American" (or "African American," which accentuates the "African" by dropping the hyphen) implies a degree of dual national self-identification, as does "Italian-American" or "Chinese-American." Moreover, the "African-American" label fails to identify directly with the slave culture, since its reference is to preslavery times. Middle-class and upper-class Blacks prefer this term because it distances them from the slave past.

"African-American" is also more acceptable to most whites, among whom a large majority is in denial of the realities of slavery—that crime against humanity that used to be referred to euphemistically as America's "peculiar institution." Moreover, an even greater majority of white Americans denies the obvious fact that the outgrowths of slavery still affect our contemporary society. These features are manifested as consequences of the century-long second-class citizenship imposed upon the newly freed slaves between the end of the Civil War in 1865 and the passage of the Civil Rights Act of 1965 one hundred years later.

■ ■ ■

Today's United States civic culture is based on the traditions of the "melting pot," which was designed by the Anglo-Saxon Protestant elite for successive waves of immigrants . The purpose of this institution was to assimilate all other ethnic cultures into Anglo-Saxon Protestant culture—to transform ethnic groups into "honorary Anglo-Saxons." Blacks were excluded from the melting pot on the false ground that they had no distinct culture and therefore did not merit "ethnic" status.

As a consequence of this policy, Blacks were assigned the status of a "racial minority" and classified as second-class "colored" citizens (note the lower-case *c*). Today, the official racial-minority classification remains in force. This status has always been below "immigrant," and consequently immigrants, including those belonging to "racial minorities," are given preference over Black Americans whose ancestors were slaves.

United States slaves were forcibly transported here, primarily from West and Central Africa, and they forged a common culture out of the cultures of many tribes. Their common language evolved as an adaptation of English currently referred to as "Black English." This Black cultural tradition continues to be preserved and developed. It differs significantly from the varied cultures of African-American descendants of immigrants who were able to preserve their original cultures intact. The United States institutional infrastructure exploits this cultural difference between Blacks and African-American descendants of immigrants by pitting these two groups against one another.

An example of this ploy can be found in the recent disclosure that most African-American students in predominantly white institutions of higher learning have been drawn from the relatively small minority that is descended from immigrants. By contrast, the overwhelming majority of students in predominantly Black institutions of higher learning are descended from slaves.

In this manner, "African-Americans" have been officially divided into a higher class of immigrant-descended African-Americans and a lower class of slave-descended African-Americans. The apparently accurate, respectful, capitalized, inclusive, and unifying self-identification "African-American" conceals a caste division. The self-identification "Black" asserts cultural distinctiveness but rejects identification with any foreign nation.

Thus, labels are significant because they reflect the cultural politics of the time.

■　■　■

When the civil rights revolution overthrew legal segregation, second-class citizenship was abolished and all citizens, regardless of racial or national origin, were endowed with equal legal rights. On this basis, the law was deemed to be color-blind. However, since United States citizens are still officially classified by race, the premise of a "color-blind" society conceals racial bias. The vast majority of Blacks know from experience that the United States is the most color-conscious nation in the world. Color prejudice, misnamed "racial prejudice," permeates every pore of United States society and remains a universal institutional disease.

It is in this context that the identification *Black* takes on added significance. With its capital *B*, it asserts *both* a group identity *and* an identity with the darkest members of the group having Southern field-slave ancestors.

While today's identification labels are primarily "Black" and "African-American," prior to the civil rights movement of the 1960s, "Negro" was well on the way toward displacing "Colored" as the generally accepted identification. The Black revolution triggered by Rev. Martin Luther King, Jr.'s Montgomery, Alabama bus boycott completed that process with a few exceptions, the most significant of which was the liberal National Association for the Advancement of Colored People. Its name went hand in hand with its moderate policies and predominantly middle-class and upper-class membership, setting it apart from the more militant Black organizations that had a working-class base.

During the early stages of the civil rights movement, the moderate national leadership of the NAACP opposed Rev. King's progressive program of nonviolent mass action and did not support him until compelled to do so by its own rank-and-file membership. To this day, the NAACP has steadfastly clung to its outdated name.

The historic Civil Rights Act of 1965 marked a significant advance, ending legal segregation, but did little more than legalize the entry of individual middle-class Blacks into a melting pot that had excluded them for a hundred years. This proved to be not nearly enough. Since the gains won by the civil rights movement benefited the Black middle class and professionals without substantially helping the great majority who constituted the Black working class and poor, the next phase of the Black freedom struggle was more militant and was led by the working class.

It is against this background that the late 1960s and the 1970s bore witness to the dramatic rise of the Black Power movement that aimed at taking an equitable share of political power "by the means necessary," including armed self-defense and local community control of the police. At its height, this movement won a broad base, extending from Rev. Martin Luther King's Poor People's March through Black soldiers' opposition to the Vietnam War to the Black Panther Party. It spawned many local independent groups, such as the Oakland Black Panthers and the Southern-based Deacons for Defense, and it revived Black caucuses in labor unions. It was one of the main factors that inspired Malcolm X to leave the Nation of Islam in search of a broader base.

The "white backlash" of the 1970s was a direct response to the Black Power movement, and President Richard Nixon exploited it with his "Southern Strategy" to win the elections of 1968 and 1972. Once in office, he unleashed the United States intelligence community to prosecute a relentless and illegal secret war of attrition against the leadership of the Black Power movement.

After eight years of Ronald Reagan and four years of George Bush had greatly eroded the gains of both civil rights and cultural revolutions of the 1960s, Bill Clinton's victory in the 1992 presidential election ushered in the middle-class-oriented "culture wars" of the 1990s. As was the case with the earlier civil rights movement, the Black middle class gained significantly from "diversity" in academia and in the corporate infrastructure. The Black working class was largely left out.

■ ■ ■

It is through my personal experience and the collective historical experience of Black Americans that I perceive the reality of America and compare it with the illusions fostered by America's ruling elite.

America's current ruling class is dominated by a group of wealthy English-Americans and German-Americans (Anglo-Saxons, or "WASPs") who share common cultural traditions and a common Protestant religion. Most of the Founding Fathers who wrote the Constitution of the United States belonged to this ethnic group, and virtually all of them were large-scale property owners. Many of them owned slaves. Their socioeconomic priorities, ideology, and political principles still guide our public life, even though the Constitution they wrote has been significantly amended.

They define the "American Dream" of rags to riches, upward mobility for everyone. Property is valued above people. Human rights are superseded by civil (legal) rights. The interests of the individual are deemed more important than the interests of the community. These values, opposite to those of Black Americans, provided the basis for the original Constitution's toleration of slavery. Thus, although Black Americans as a people abide by the United States Constitution, most of us have scant faith in it.

The Declaration of Independence and the Constitution of the United States were written at a time when, according to the Census of 1790, the United States population was approximately 3.95 million people: 3 million whites, 50,000 free Blacks, and 900,000 Black slaves. Native Americans were not counted as persons unless they paid taxes. Black slaves were counted as three-fifths of a person for the purpose of assigning representation from the States in the Congress. However, all whites, including indentured servants, were counted as "free persons" (full citizens).

Since Black slaves had no rights, only the 50,000 Black freedmen, or 5.3 percent of the total Black population, were citizens. Moreover, since in practice only white male property owners were originally allowed to vote, a majority of the white population was also disenfranchised. The first ten Amendments to the Constitution (the "Bill of Rights" adopted in 1791) still did not give women the right to vote. Only in 1920 did the nineteenth Amendment extend voting rights to women.

The Preamble of the Constitution is written in general language that is subject to interpretation. It is short:

> We the People of the United States, in Order to form a more perfect Union, establish Justice, insure domestic Tranquility, provide for the common defence, promote the general Welfare, and secure the Blessings of Liberty to ourselves and our Posterity, do ordain and establish this Constitution for the United States of America.

Based on the Constitution's definition of citizenship and voting rights, "We the People" does *not* mean all human beings inhabiting the United States. It is restricted to persons who have citizenship rights (or "civil rights"); there is no mention of *human* rights. At the time the Constitution was written, Black slaves, constituting almost 25 percent of the total United States population and deprived of full human status, were victims of a crime against humanity.

Native Americans, denied human status entirely, were subjected to one of the largest genocidal "ethnic cleansing" campaigns in recorded history. This issue is a personal one for me, since, like a significant number of Black Americans of slave ancestry, I have Native American ancestors on my paternal grandmother's side.

Thus, the men who wrote the United States Constitution were complicit in two crimes against humanity.

The language of the Declaration of Independence is similarly restrictive. The statement that, "all men are created equal . . . [and] are endowed by their Creator with certain unalienable rights, that among these, are life, liberty and the pursuit of happiness" does not apply to slaves, Native Americans, or women. The Declaration stresses "liberty" but makes no mention of "freedom." It could not have used the word *freedom* without directly confronting the issue of slavery as the ultimate denial of *liberty*. Therefore, the word "freedom" was omitted.

Thus "liberty" and "freedom" acquired differing meanings in American political discourse. Liberty meant the privileges to which the elite minority was entitled. Freedom meant the protection of all human beings, including Black slaves and Native Americans, from oppression or unfair treatment.

President Abraham Lincoln eliminated this ambiguity when he reframed the Constitution and the Declaration of Independence in his Gettysburg Address. He defined the Union as a nation "conceived in liberty," but "dedicated . . . to a new birth of freedom." This juxtaposition of liberty and freedom gave freedom the dominant place and placed federal power above states' rights. His "government of the people, by the people, for the people" meant that "we the people" included *all citizens*, including the newly freed slaves.

It still did *not* include women, who were relegated to second-class citizenship without the right to vote. However, women were counted as citizens for the purpose of allocating electoral votes to the states.

Native Americans were still not considered to be citizens at all. Rarely is it mentioned that a cruel irony is attached to their total exclusion from the Constitution of their own nation. For it is from the Iroquois Confederation that the early white colonists learned their legendary political insistence on limited government and their long-standing cultural disdain for elites. The Confederation was governed by the Great Law of Peace—a Constitution consisting of 117 codicils that established a Great Council of fifty male religious-political leaders, each representing one of the female-led clans of the Confederation's nations. Every "important matter or great emergency" had to be submitted to a referendum open to both men and women.

It is no exaggeration to say that the Native American political tradition served as the wellspring of the American commitment to liberty. New Hampshire's motto, "Live Free or Die," stems from the Native Americans' determined choice of resistance to the death in preference to slavery. The American colonists at the Boston Tea Party dressed as Mohawks. The early suffragettes were inspired by the Great Law's stipulation of legal protections for women.

Moreover, the legacy of the Great Law reached far beyond America's shores. Friedrich Engels, cofounder with Karl

Marx of the Communist movement, extolled the Great Law's curbs on state power: "[T]his ... constitution is wonderful." Over the past two decades, some of the protesters demanding liberty in South Korea, China and the Ukraine wore Native American makeup and dress.

Black culture differed significantly from the culture of liberty and individualism—the opportunity for every individual to do anything reasonable that they wished to do. The slave culture was about a quest for freedom from oppression and for community advancement. Unlike Native Americans, the African slaves were an imprisoned minority in an alien land. Instead of choosing death in the face of continued enslavement, the slaves found ways to survive while preserving their culture. On the other hand, Native Americans chose to face death rather than enslavement in their own land.

Black Americans' post-Lincoln icon is President Franklin D. Roosevelt with his historic "Four Freedoms": Freedom *from* fear, Freedom *from* want, Freedom *of* speech, and Freedom *of* religion. Most Black Americans identify the first two as freedoms and the second two as liberties. Roosevelt's sequence establishes his priorities, which are the same as Lincoln's: freedom has priority over liberty.

Black Americans are freedom people rather than liberty people. We gather at the Lincoln Memorial, rather than at the Jefferson Memorial. We view *Conservatives* as the heirs of the Confederacy and *Progressives* as the heirs of the Union. We see two Americas—Conservative America and Progressive America. Most of us identify with Progressive America and oppose Conservative America. For us, the states in our nation are symbolically colored Blue for the Union and Gray for the Confederacy. We don't see any "Red" States, since Red is the symbolic designation for Communism and Socialism.

When the delegates to the 1788 Constitutional Convention ratified the Constitution, the dominant centrist faction imposed a compromise document that bridged the gap between those who demanded a confederacy and those who insisted on a union. The Preamble of the Constitution proclaimed the goal of "a more perfect Union," but the Articles defined a kind of Union-Confederacy, with the balance tipped slightly toward the Union. The strong Confederate influence is most obvious in the failure of the Constitution to abolish slavery, its definition of a slave as three-fifths of a person in order to increase the Congressional representation of the Southern States, and its guarantee of States' rights.

Today, this usually dominant centrist tradition is considered to be bipartisan and called Liberal. However, a strong majority of Black Americans supports a partisan Progressive agenda and rejects the Liberal program. Therefore, since usually the only electoral choice is between a Liberal and a Conservative, most Black voters consistently vote *against* the Conservative whose agenda we perceive to be contrary to our vital interests. The only candidates most of us vote *for* are Progressives.

In my view, today's national divide is the same as it has been since the founding of our Republic—a conflict between Progressives and Conservatives over fundamental values. The middle ground is vanishing, and "bipartisanship" is doomed to failure. Against this background, it is in the interests of the vast majority of Blacks, as a vital component of Progressive America, to defeat Conservative America decisively. Our core values are in harmony with the principal Progressive values but conflict sharply with many Conservative ones.

■ ■ ■

My personal value system differs from the one taught by the traditional United States civic culture and is based on six main civic principles. They were passed on to me by my father, the son of an escaped field slave.

1. *Strive for excellence; try to be the best that you can possibly be. Aim for perfection instead of merely trying to "beat" others.*

This principle challenges the civic culture's unhealthy obsession with winning at any cost. It presents a stark contrast to the grotesque popular slogan: "Winning is not only everything; it is the only thing."

2. *Success without advancing the interests of our people as a whole, without helping those who have fallen behind, is worth little.*

This admonition reflects a communitarian tradition according to which the general welfare of the community as a whole is as important as individual advancement. It teaches outright rejection of the "radical individualism" that serves as the main pillar of America's traditional mainstream culture and undermines commitment to community interests.

3. *The human race is one family, with diverse but equal members having different cultures, and a deeper understanding of one's own culture will inevitably lead to a better understanding of other cultures.*

This rejection of the very idea that "race matters" in any intrinsically human sense reflects the deeply rooted ecumenicalism and universalism of the shared culture of Southern slaves. I believe that the so-called "race issue" in the

United States has been fashioned into the primary tool with which the ruling Anglo-Saxon Protestant ethnic group divides and dominates the remainder of the population.

Virtually all of the field slaves, as well as many skilled slaves and house slaves, rejected the color-based caste system of their masters. Originating from a broad array of African tribes and nations, they also rejected the exclusionary features of nationalism and tribalism in favor of developing a collective culture while preserving its distinct tribal and national components.

4. *Personal growth is the mother of greatness, but its price is pain and perseverance.*

A high level of communally nurtured personal growth was required for the slaves to preserve their humanity in the face of the extremely antihuman conditions imposed on them by slavery. Today, many young people of all ethnic groups mistakenly seek instant success, riches, and celebrity.

5. *Temper strength and power with gentleness and compassion; balance courage with wisdom.*

This cautionary advice repudiates the arrogant, reckless, macho attitude currently marketed so assiduously by the United States civic culture. It also harbors an implicit, concealed message: "Make love, not war. And if you must fight, do so wisely and try to live to fight another day."

6. *Don't go along to get along. Be willing to sacrifice to do what you know is right.*

This last principle places dedication to principle far ahead of personal opportunism. Its importance has been accentuated by today's headlines describing pervasive corruption, deceit, and compromise.

These Black ethical guidelines differ from the operative values of most whites and of a significant number (albeit a relatively small minority) of Blacks. They are rarely, if ever, discussed in depth in any segment of the media, including "alternative" media and Black media. Their source is rooted in intuition based on experience, rather than in intellectual reasoning based on personal gratification and financial gain.

Any serious discussion of Black culture must include the essence of Black religious tradition. Today Black religious institutions, though nominally Protestant and officially governed according to the precepts of the New Testament, King James Version, are separate from and independent of white Protestant religious institutions.

Black culture is rooted in spiritual faith rather than in formal religious teachings. Our faith-based religion derives from our selective interpretation of the King James Version of the New Testament because that was the only book that slaves were legally permitted to read. Our ancestors forged their interpretation of that book into a powerful weapon against the culture of slavery. They chose and wove together the allusions to the ancient Hebrew heroes and heroines—the "freedom fighters" and scholars who lived prior to the writing of even the Old Testament.

These legends were integrated into the tapestry of music and dance that is reflected in the spirituals, gospel songs, ring dances, folk music, and folk tales that constitute the core of the slave culture. This tradition pays little attention to the numerous saints in the New Testament, which is treated as a metaphorical text rather than as a literal set of rules.

Our key religious figure is *Jesus of Nazareth* (as distinct from "Jesus Christ"), the great Hebrew prophet who was rooted in the ancient Hebraic tradition and personified the *Divine Spirit* that inhabits every human being. His assertion,

"I am the way," was taken to mean that faith in his teachings would lead all people to the Divine Spirit within themselves. Jesus, the champion of the meek and the poor, the symbol of peaceful challenge to the rich and powerful, the martyr who conquered death with faith, was our patron saint.

Today, a decisive majority of Blacks are still people of redemptive, inclusive faith—"Jesus people"—rather than people of judgmental, exclusive faith. Therefore, we are *Judeo-Christians*, as distinct from those who call themselves *exclusively Christian*. And, in my view, the sharpest religious division in the United States today is between *fundamentalist Christians* and *universalist Judeo-Christians*.

■ ■ ■

In the chapters that follow, I will examine six different controversial issues, from the perception of the 9/11 terrorist attacks to the exercise of Black political power. I view these issues from a Black perspective, based on a perception of reality that differs vastly from the false illusions propagated incessantly by the mass media and the national leadership. I will attempt to describe reality as I perceive it, foregoing the civic culture's unwritten rule that political debate must conform to official myths.

My Black worldview rejects those myths, and the following chapters attempt to expose the falsity of their premises and the ambiguity of the words with which they are propagated. I discuss the contradictions in American society that underlie the reality of two Americas rather than one. Like other Black Americans, I know from experience that the United States is not a land of "liberty and justice for all." I have learned that official propaganda seeks to represent this admirable but distant goal as existing reality.

For example, we are a republic rather than a "democracy." Our two-party, bipartisan political system, with its winner-take-all principle and electoral college for electing presidents, is designed to prevent direct popular control. At the same time, however, the commendable separation of governmental powers tends to forestall the imposition of a dictatorship by a ruling administration.

In our current political environment, the rules of public discourse are finely controlled by the official culture and its mass media through the coded meanings of ambiguous words.

For instance, changes in ethnic labels harbor subtle meanings that entail significant social and political consequences.

In the 1790s the ruling elite, who were mainly descendants of Protestant English and German colonists, called themselves "New Aryans." Later, they adopted the "WASP" self-identification: *White* Anglo-Saxon Protestant. Since "Anglo-Saxon" already means white, "White Anglo-Saxon" means double-white, or super-white. "WASP" subsequently gave way to "American," a self-identification that conceals ethnicity entirely.

Consequently, those white descendants of immigrants who chose to assimilate into WASP culture likewise adopted the self-identification "American." This process of massive cultural assimilation of non-WASP whites has left African Americans, Asian Americans, Native Americans, and Latino Americans as unassimilatable "minorities" who are distinct from the white majority.

The majority of Latinos that has the option of a "white" self-identification is being intensively pressured by the WASP establishment to assimilate into the white majority. The purpose of this campaign is to neutralize independent Latino political power. So far, the results have been meager.

The "racial minorities"—who consist of African Americans, Asian Americans, nonwhite Latinos, and Native Americans—are being offered a semiassimilation contingent on *class*. Stressing the fiction that the 1965 Civil Rights Act created a "color-blind" society because it abolished *legal* racial discrimination, "racial minorities" are told by the gatekeepers of the mainstream culture that their adoption of middle-class WASP values will guarantee their complete assimilation. The offer has been buttressed by countless individual "role models."

At the same time, all of the minorities are pitted against one another. For example, Latinos with a white self-identification are favored over those who choose to retain their identification with Latino culture. African Americans of immigrant descent are favored over Blacks with Southern slave ancestors. In addition, the very concept of a "minority" has been confused by the false classification of all women, who actually constitute a majority of the total population, as members of a "minority."

■ ■ ■

The official language of the national political discourse is full of encoded references, distortions, and falsifications, all of which ultimately derive from the contradictions written into the Constitution of the United States and the Declaration of Independence.

The essays that follow attempt to present a coherent picture of the current cultural, economic, and political aims of the majority of Black Americans, using language and metaphors emanating from the Black experience. I deliberately avoid using the false labels, misleading language, and deceptive metaphors that have been injected into the national debate about race by the WASP-dominated cultural establishment.

While honoring Black cultural traditions, I do not hesitate to break current Black political conventions. I aim to expose the conflicts within the Black community. I name political enemies and friends on both the domestic and foreign scenes. And I discuss openly the strengths and weaknesses of the current Black political establishment.

We Black Americans live in a different reality than white Americans. We are treated differently, and we perceive the world differently; we share a distinct set of cultural, economic, and personal values. Many white Americans feel threatened when we act as ourselves. They require that we behave in a more familiar stereotypical manner. However, most of us have grown tired of this nuanced charade that has replaced the cruder "minstrel show."

A majority of us, especially those born after the civil rights revolution of the 1960s, are determined to live and act according to our own cultural traditions and to pursue our own interests in our own way. In this fundamental sense, we are claiming our full place as equal Americans in a United States that we, as much as any group, have helped to build.

CHAPTER I

9/11 IN BLACK AND WHITE

Like most Black New Yorkers at the beginning of September 2001, I was looking forward to Mayor Rudy Giuliani's imminent departure from office. With eight years of constant race baiting, he had divided New York City's Black and white communities more than any other mayor who had held office during the fifty-two years I had lived here. He disliked African-Americans, and we disliked him.

Suddenly, on September 11, New York City was subjected to a monumental terrorist attack that killed three thousand New Yorkers. Saudi Arabian hijackers flew two commercial airliners into the World Trade Center Twin Towers, causing them to burn and collapse. New Yorkers as a whole responded to this disaster as one enormous family. We reached out to one another, suffered together, mourned together. Our normally noisy, hardboiled, racially polarized city became hushed and contemplative as it absorbed the enormity of what had happened to it.

However, under the leadership of Mayor Giuliani, this positive mood dissipated rapidly. As the days went on, he toured the city with a virtually all-white retinue, busily reassuring whites while generally avoiding Black neighborhoods and never mentioning the name of C. Virginia Fields, the Black borough president of Manhattan who had played a key role in organizing the herculean emergency and recovery efforts. Instead, he elbowed her out of television camera range along with any other Black or Latino officials who were nearby.

The media studiously avoided mentioning the obvious, and Black leaders acted as if they hadn't noticed. Meanwhile, Giuliani played to an adoring press. At virtually every one of his photo-ops, the Mayor was flanked by Fire Commissioner Thomas Von Essen, who paraded under the Mayor's undeserved imprimatur as intrepid leader of the heroic firefighters. The reality had been far different, since both of these men had failed their respective tests of leadership.

Videotapes show Von Essen in Mayor Giuliani's command bunker in Tower Number 7, helplessly watching the chaos and confusion surrounding him. Neither he nor the Mayor provided leadership to the heroic but uncoordinated efforts of the army of firefighters, rescue workers, medical teams, policemen, and volunteers selflessly risking their lives in the hell of Ground Zero. Hundreds of firemen were driven up the tower stairs to the high floors in accordance with a prior set of instructions unrelated to the actual conditions they would face. Adding to their vulnerability, their communication devices failed to work properly inside the buildings—an inexcusable handicap since the firefighters had been complaining about this life-threatening hazard for months. If the devices had been functional, they could have been ordered back downstairs.

Over 350 firefighters died that day, including a large proportion of the higher ranks, who shared the same dangers as the men and women they commanded. At least 200 of these heroes may have perished unnecessarily because of the colossal incompetence of Fire Commissioner Thomas Von Essen and the lack of leadership manifested by Mayor Giuliani.

A January 30, 2002, article in the *New York Times* reported that the Fire Department's most senior commanders "had little reliable radio communication on 9/11, could not keep track of all the firefighters who entered the towers, and were unable to reach them as the threat of a collapse became unmistakable." One chief "estimated that at the moment the North Tower fell, nearly every civilian below the floors hit by the airplane had already been evacuated, and that only firefighters remained inside the stairwells of a building that was seen as a lost cause." A city engineer's warning that the Towers were about to collapse could not reach the highest-ranking fire chief by radio.[1]

As commander in chief, the Mayor's primary job was to assemble all of the operational commanders to create a new collective plan of action in the face of this unforeseen disaster. This should have been done immediately after the first aircraft struck. Moreover, given the obviously unpredictable consequences of the impact on the structure of the Towers, the World Trade Center command post should have been moved to a safer place immediately after the first tower was hit. Instead, Giuliani, concerned with making a public appearance on the streets, departed from the bunker minutes before an avalanche of falling debris killed everyone remaining inside.

Soon after, the Fire Commissioner and the Mayor presided over a virtually all-white ceremony that inducted hundreds of new firefighters and promoted many others to the higher ranks in order to fill the enormous gaps left behind by the martyrs of 9/11. Hardly any Black faces, Latino faces, or female faces. The Mayor's implied message was clear: We have a virtually lily-white Fire Department, and we're going to keep it that way. Most white New Yorkers did not seem disturbed by this; they appeared to ignore it all.[2]

■ ■ ■

On October 8, 2001, *The New Yorker* magazine encapsulated the media's "Great White Father" Giuliani image:

> He was unstintingly *there*—at the scene, so close that he was nearly killed when the first tower collapsed. His demeanor—calm, frank, patient, tender, egoless, competent—was, as carried to the city and the world through the intimacy of television, profoundly reassuring. He displayed all the right emotions, and he displayed them in just the right way, often by keeping them in check. "City Fathers" is an old-fashioned term, seldom used anymore except with a hint of derision. But Giuliani, during this terrible time, has truly been the city's father—strong and kind, firm and comforting.

The political windfall of 9/11 inflated Giuliani into the hero-mayor of the hero-city. On a national scale, it enabled President George W. Bush's conservative Republican Party to exploit the tragedy for the purpose of consolidating and extending its power at all levels of American political life. The theme was unity. Voicing minority opinions was assailed as divisive and therefore unpatriotic.

However, the preceding week, a September 30, 2001 editorial in the *New York Times* had sounded a far different note, warning that America's mood suffered from an air of unreality. It openly criticized the popular culture's "false" pandering to Americans' "vain" desire for elimination of our nation's "inherent dissensions," to their need for "good-humored, inoffensive escapism," and to their naive denial of "irony" and "cynicism":

A sudden sensitivity to the psychic wounds inflicted by that disastrous morning was movingly evident everywhere. Radio stations reconsidered their hard rock playlists, excising a cultural rage that suddenly looked calculated. These gestures were made in the spirit of patriotic unity, and they were made as ingenuously as the entertainment industry could make them. For a moment, all the disharmonies, all the inherent dissensions in our culture—all the things that actually make it a culture—were stilled in a nearly unanimous expression of grief, respect and outrage.

But America cannot live in the unanimity of that moment, nor should it expect to, no matter how attractive it looks.

Everyone craved safety and consolation in strong doses after the attack, and the predictors of our cultural future suggested that in the months ahead, we would need as much good-humored inoffensive escapism as we could find. But those predictions are themselves an artifact of the moment, the expression of a desire that is cousin to the fear we all felt and continue to feel. Irony is unchanged by the terrorist attack, for it is still a modality that America barely understands. Cynicism runs exactly skin deep, as always. The only difference in the entertainment offered to America after September 11 will probably be the expectation that it is good for us. Behind all these cultural predictions lies the assumption that what we really need to do is to avert our eyes from what we have already watched in horror, that we need, some-how, to prevent our innocence from being further impaired by the smoke and ash and death that rained down on this country that day. That is a false, not to say a vain, assumption. The hard work of making cultural sense of those hours still lies ahead of us, for years to come, and it will not be done in a spirit of escapism or unanimity.[3]

Black Americans are a people who have experienced official and unofficial state terror, mob terror, and clandestine terror in this country for generations; we are all too familiar with it. And we rank high among the world's experts at combating the fear engendered by terrorist attacks. We also know how to fight terrorism with accurate intelligence combined with the use of both psychological warfare and counterterror in self-defense. But, of course, no one in authority thought to tap our collective experience.

The media tend to serve up mainly white images and white culture in times of trial and fear. Black images all but disappear. Reminders of America's cultural diversity vanish. A constant stream of superpatriotic, jingoistic propaganda pours endlessly from virtually every media outlet. American flags are suddenly displayed in profusion in white neighborhoods and on white-owned cars.

But we marched to a different drummer.

When I left a white community and arrived home in my predominantly Black community, I entered a different world. Few American flags were on display. People were as outraged and frightened as other Americans, but they were not terrorized by their fear. They pointedly stayed away from the patriotic rallies. From the outset, many Black Americans, if not a majority, were suspicious of the motives behind the Bush Administration's "War Against Terror" and "Homeland Security Department." Unlike most white Americans, we did not give President Bush the benefit of the doubt.

Many of us didn't believe a word he said. We assumed that his "preemptive war" doctrine, his ill-concealed contempt for the United Nations and our European allies, and his high-altitude carpet bombing of Afghanistan signaled United States military interventions to control Middle Eastern oil. The Department of Homeland Security looked more like a mechanism for suppressing internal dissent than a means for protecting the nation from terrorists. We also found a way to avoid the media's propaganda barrage by watching British and Canadian television for the news. Polls, almost all them ignored by the media, showed that most Blacks were skeptical of Bush's post-9/11 policies, whereas most whites trusted him.

Not only did Blacks mistrust Bush, most of us despised him, and we still do. We see him as a Southern racist who tries to conceal his real persona with hypocritical chatter about "compassionate conservatism" and love of liberty and freedom. Based on the exhaustive detail of *The 9/11 Commission Report* and the revealing book *Against All Enemies* by Richard Clarke, Bush's National Security Coordinator until March of 2003, some of us, including myself, believe that the Bush administration had advance warning of the 9/11 terrorist attack and deliberately let it happen in order to exploit the thousands of innocent deaths for political gain.

By now it has become obvious that the national obsession with 9/11 was artificially created with the willing collusion of mass media that were universally bought or coerced by the Bush administration and its army of Republican political thugs. Its craven subservience to state authority has been far more pervasive than it was during the so-called McCarthy era of the 1950s. It brings to mind the memorable comment by Senator Sam Ervin, a North Carolina Democrat, who said that the Nixon administration's attempted Watergate coup revealed Nixon's "Gestapo mentality."

Some of us who are familiar with European twentieth-century history, including this writer, believe that there is a similarity between the political and propaganda techniques used by the Bush administration and the totalitarian traditions personified by Hitler, Stalin, Mussolini, and Franco. The stock-in-trade of Bush, Cheney, Rove & Company consists of fear-mongering, the political smear, the unrestrained use of the Big Lie, election fraud on an unprecedented scale, unbridled nationalism, direct or subtle appeals to racial and ethnic prejudices, preventive wars to prevent a *possible* attack (as distinct from preemptive wars to preempt a *reasonably certain*, impending attack), and the cavalier flouting of any and all international conventions and treaties.

The core Bush constituency—Southern WASPs augmented by the Protestant and Catholic religious right— resembles that of Hitler, whose base was in the southern part of predominantly Anglo-Saxon ("Aryan") Germany where he attracted many right-wing Catholics. The tacit Republican endorsement of the Confederate battle flag invites a comparison with the Nazi swastika flag, and the song "Dixie" calls the Nazi "Horst Wessel" song to my mind. And not least is the analogy between the German national anthem, "Deutschland Über alles" ("Germany Above All"), and the slogan "America is Number One."

In my view, the Bush Administration is building upon the legacy of the Confederacy, of the infamous Senator Joseph McCarthy of Wisconsin, of J. Edgar Hoover's "Big Brother" FBI, of President Nixon's Watergate coup and Southern strategy, and of President Reagan's "Irangate" banditry executed by former Colonel Oliver North using Nazi-like methods. The aim appears to be nothing less than the establishment of a United States world empire in combination with totalitarian theocratic domestic rule—the First American Realm in the First American Century.

To me, this mad scheme is the nightmare cooked up in the bowels of the Department of Defense by neocons and their caricature emperor-designate George W. Bush. Karl Rove, the consummate political strategist and propagandist, respects no laws, rules, or conventions, resembling a caricature Cardinal Richelieu to Bush's Louis the Fourteenth. If the probable consequences of this escapade were not so sinister, it would be hilarious—fodder for a Chaplinesque movie titled, "The Great Dictator II: Oil Wars." However, the wholesale media betrayal of their own civic and ethical duty has converted a fantasy barely worthy of a comic strip into a poisonous reality.

The white mass media have been and remain in steadfast denial of reality when it comes to the motives and results of the Bush administration's policies. Moreover, any deviation from the official administration on any and all domestic and foreign issues is treated with skepticism at best and is censored out at worst. On the other hand, Black-controlled media outlets disseminate a full range of dissident opinions. These include mine, which are effectively banned from the mainstream media. It is for this reason that Republican money is feverishly buying up Black media entities throughout the nation and buying out those Black journalists they can corrupt.

Our response should be to reassert exclusive control of our means of public communication. Then we shall be able to conduct a meaningful public dialogue with other groups.

In themselves, Black-white cultural differences do not come close to constituting a serious divide, let alone an unbridgeable one, among ethnic groups in the United States. All Americans share many cultural traits, including a common language and a popular culture. We inhabit a common territory and a common economic space. Diverse ethnic groups in many other countries would count their blessings many times over if they were so fortunate.

I have concluded that the Black-white divide is a reflection of a systemic societal failure; it is something that cannot be addressed realistically without discussing at least the possibility of radical political and economic change. Therefore such a discussion is a prerequisite for a constructive public discourse on race. It is also the sole route toward a more unified nation.

NOTES

1. "Before the Towers Fell, Fire Dept. Fought Chaos," *New York Times*, January 30, 2002.
2. The front page of the *New York Times* of August 13, 2003, displayed a photograph of the graduation-day ceremony for 346 probationary New York City firefighters, "the largest group ever to complete training." It showed the seated ranks of the firefighters and hundreds of their family members in the audience. Even with a high-power magnifying glass, I had difficulty finding a single Black face in the sea of white ones.
3. "Cultural Predictions in the Wake of the Terrorist Attack," *New York Times*, September 30, 2001.

CHAPTER II

EIGHT COUPS IN
AMERICAN HISTORY

Americans tend to be captives of the myth that political coups occur only in Third World countries. Many are unaware that George W. Bush became president as the result of a sophisticated coup by the Republican Party. Those who engineered the coup consummated the process begun by President Nixon and developed by President Reagan, and they have completed the 140-year transformation of the Republican Party from the party of Lincoln to one that wears the states'-rights mantle of Confederate President Jefferson Davis and defers to the Confederate battle flag.

Bush's Republican Party speaks for a racist, right-wing Southern constituency and its white, conservative Northern allies. It has become so racist that J. C. Watts, Congress's sole Black Republican and chairman of the House Republican Conference, has returned to private life instead of remaining in his post as a Republican congressional leader. Today no African-American elected on a Republican ticket sits in Congress.

George W. Bush's mission in the White House is to establish nationwide a modern version of the old Confederacy based on the New South. In pursuing it, he is building on the foundation created by six previous Southern-based, states-rights coups.

The first Confederate coup assassinated President Abraham Lincoln in Washington, D.C. and derailed Reconstruction in the South. The right-wing WASP conspiracy that carried out this evil act of domestic terrorism was hatched by Confederates, their Northern supporters, and Canadian and British intelligence agents. Seven people were tried, convicted and hung for the crime, yet most historical texts imply that a single assassin named John Wilkes Booth killed Lincoln.

The conspirators' motive was to prevent Lincoln from carrying out his Reconstruction policy based on the unconditional surrender of the Confederacy. This policy was foreshadowed by the following passage in his 1865 Inaugural Address:

> Fondly do we hope, fervently do we pray, that this mighty scourge of war may speedily pass away. Yet if God wills that it continue until all the wealth piled by the bondsman's two hundred and fifty years of unrequited toil shall be sunk, and until every drop of blood drawn with the lash shall be paid by another drawn with the sword, as was said three thousand years ago, so still it must be said, "The judgements of the Lord are true and righteous altogether."

Lincoln's assassination cleared the way for the presidency of Vice President Andrew Johnson of the Southern border state of Missouri, who could be counted on to betray Lincoln's policy by blocking federal enforcement of the civil rights of freed slaves. Although President Johnson escaped impeachment by only one vote on the minor technical charge of illegally appointing a cabinet member, one of the underlying reasons for his attempted impeachment was suspicion of treason and complicity in the plot to kill Lincoln. There was also strong but inconclusive evidence that a cabinet member, as well as high-ranking military and intelligence personnel, were directly involved in the conspiracy.

The second coup, engineered almost a hundred years later, was the assassination of President John F. Kennedy in Dallas, Texas. This act of terror was carried out by the heirs of the right-wing Southern WASP conspiracy that assassinated Lincoln; it stemmed from essentially the same motivations. The goal was to thwart President Kennedy's intention to complete the aborted post–Civil War Reconstruction and to transform the United States political system into Lincoln's "government of the people, by the people, for the people."[1]

Similarly, the real story behind Kennedy's assassination has been covered up by the persistently marketed fiction of a single assassin—Lee Harvey Oswald.

Kennedy's program was clear. In a nationwide address on June 11, 1963, Kennedy embraced the joint goals of legislating federally enforced civil rights *and* economic rights. As the civil rights movement unfolded, Kennedy declared that Black Americans remained politically, socially, and *economically* oppressed:

> One hundred years of delay have passed since President Lincoln freed the slaves, yet their heirs, their grandsons, are not fully free. They are not yet freed from the bonds of injustice. They are not yet freed from social and economic oppression. . . . We are confronted primarily with a moral issue. It is as old as the scriptures and is as clear as the American Con-

stitution. The heart of the question is whether all Americans are to be afforded equal rights and equal opportunities. . . . Now the time has come for this nation to fulfill its promise.

The promise of which Kennedy spoke includes a clear commitment to equal opportunity, not merely to civil rights. A year earlier, he had left no doubt about his will to protect civil rights in the South with armed force. He had ordered 20,000 regular-army troops with live ammunition to disperse the violent mob that had converged on the University of Mississippi campus in an attempt to prevent James Meredith from entering the University as its first Black student.

Kennedy spoke to both national and international policy. In his inaugural address, he invoked President Franklin D. Roosevelt's New Deal commitment to empower the poor: "If a free society cannot help the many who are poor, it cannot save the few who are rich." Then he went on to reject both the cherished right-wing shibboleth of world domination through military power and the conservative distrust of the United Nations:

Let the word go forth that the torch has been passed to a new generation of Americans, proud of our ancient heritage. . . . To that world assembly of sovereign states—the United Nations, our last best hope—we renew our pledge to prevent it from becoming merely a forum, to strengthen its shield of the new and the weak, and to enlarge the area in which its writ may run.

Let [us] . . . formulate serious and precise proposals for the inspection and control of arms, and bring the absolute power to destroy other nations under the absolute control of all nations.

Now the trumpet summons us again—not as a call to bear arms . . . ; not as a call to battle . . . ; but a call to . . . struggle against the common enemies of man: tyranny, poverty, disease and war itself.

This passage endures as an eloquent challenge to the core ideological precepts of the United States conservative tradition; it was considered to be "treason" by the right-wing WASP conspiracy.

Partially repeating history, Kennedy was succeeded by a vice president from the Southern border state of Texas, Lyndon Johnson. Although Johnson had no intention of reversing Kennedy's announced policies, it was well known that he opposed the radical reforms Kennedy had signaled he would champion in his second term. These goals had been foreshadowed in several of President Kennedy's major speeches.

■　■　■

Ten years later, President Richard Nixon's Watergate scandal was a brazen attempt to impose a presidential dictatorship based on the Republican Party's Southern Strategy. Senator Sam Ervin, a North Carolina Democrat, accused the Nixon administration of harboring "a Gestapo mentality," dramatically attesting to Nixon's fascist tendencies.

General Alexander Haig, who was briefly in charge at the White House during the Watergate crisis, made comments that were interpreted by some as an implied threat to mount a military coup to maintain Nixon in power. He backed off from his remarks immediately when a majority of both civilian and military leaders supported the impeachment process. In this case, the conspiracy was isolated and defeated in advance of any attempted violence. However, its network remained intact, and as in the cases of the Lincoln and Kennedy assassinations, its existence was deliberately concealed from the United States public.

We should remember Watergate as the third Confederate coup.

The next elected Republican president, Ronald Reagan, deliberately set out to destroy the public sector of the national economy by instituting huge tax cuts for the wealthy and running up a multitrillion-dollar national debt. His goal was to make federal public spending virtually impossible for any other purpose than national defense. In pursuit of this goal, he deliberately created at least a trillion-dollar national deficit in order to cripple the federal government. This conscious sabotage of the national economy is confirmed in detail in a book by Reagan's own budget director.[2] For this alone he should have been impeached. Instead, he was enshrined as a Great Communicator.

Reagan's Confederate values were confirmed when he opened his 1980 campaign for the presidency with a speech in support of states' rights in Philadelphia, Mississippi, site of the torture and murder of three young civil rights workers in 1964. His illegal purposes became evident during the Iran-Contra scandal, when he repeatedly lied to the American people and to Congress about his arms-for-hostages deal with the Iranian fundamentalists. Colonel Oliver North, his personal agent in the Iran-Contra scandal, was compared by

World War II hero Senator Daniel Inouye to the Nazi war criminals tried at Nuremberg.

Reagan's policies during his two terms as president were dictated by the Conspiracy and constituted the successful fourth Confederate coup.

The fifth Confederate coup, perpetrated during the term of President George H. W. Bush, was legal. This Republican president, a former director of the Central Intelligence Agency, participated in the cover-up of the Iran-Contra scandal and subsequently used the first Persian Gulf War to achieve a partial revival of Nixon's imperial presidency. His successful nomination of Clarence Thomas, a Black American who believes in the Confederate principle of states' rights, to the United States Supreme Court tilted the Court decisively to the right.

Judge Thomas, like Presidents Nixon, Reagan, and George H. W. Bush, built his career as an agent of the Conspiracy. The extraordinary effectiveness of the Conspiracy is based on the total invisibility of its top leadership and on the fiction that it does not exist. Its public goals and actions are consistent with traditional conservative values, and its rhetoric echoes time-honored nationalistic slogans. The core constituency drawn to it is the culturally homogeneous Anglo-Saxon middle class and the nonunion working class.

Upon his nomination, Thomas, despite his Black working-class roots, publicly identified himself with the cultural values of this constituency while rejecting Black culture. Asserting that Blacks were merely an "interest group in a coalition supporting expanded government," he insisted that "the Constitution be interpreted in color-blind fashion" despite his acknowledgment that United States society cannot be color-blind.

This position means that, although American society is racist, Black people are merely individuals of color rather than an ethnic group and thus merit no special protection under the Constitution. Ironically, the mass media, which were and remain thoroughly infiltrated by the Conspiracy, marketed Thomas as a self-made southern Black who would add "diversity" to the Court. Republican Senator Arlen Specter of Pennsylvania echoed this phony propaganda sale when he said of Thomas:

> I think he brings a very, very important measure of diversity to the Court. I think it's very important that an African-American be on the Court now, within the chambers of the nine Justices; that they hear the views of African-Americans in this country.

Retiring Justice Thurgood Marshall, the first Black Supreme Court Justice, reflected the largely unreported views of the majority of Blacks when he dismissed Clarence Thomas as "a snake."

Thus, the fifth Confederate coup was the subversion of the United States Supreme Court during the Bush Sr. administration.

■ ■ ■

Only two post-WW II presidents have warned the nation against the Conspiracy.

The first was Dwight Eisenhower who did so indirectly on two occasions. In 1956, at the end of his first term, he ridiculed one of the main points of the Conspiracy's agenda—the idea of preemptive war: "In this day and time. . . . I don't believe there is such a thing; and, frankly, I wouldn't even listen to anyone seriously that came in and talked about it." In 1960, at the end of his second term, he alerted the nation to the internal threat emanating from "the military-industrial complex," a euphemism for the military-industrial arm of the Conspiracy.

President Bill Clinton was far more direct. In the wake of the terrorist bombing of the Oklahoma City Federal Building, he gave a speech honoring the hundreds of victims. He pinned responsibility for the outrage on a terrorist network linked to "the right-wing conspiracy." The media arm of the Conspiracy immediately launched a vile stream of invective against the President in a largely successful effort to counter his public exposure of the political link between the extreme right and domestic terrorism.

I do not believe that the questionable FBI investigation of the terrorist bombing, which involved the disappearance of a large number of documents and was never reviewed by Congress, had anything to do with incompetence. On the contrary, I believe that the FBI, on instructions from the Conspiracy, executed a skillful cover-up of the links between the political extreme right and domestic terrorism.

The anti-Clinton witch hunt spearheaded by Kenneth Starr was launched by the agents of the Conspiracy, and when First Lady Hillary Clinton accurately connected the dots in this matter, the mass media successfully ridiculed her.

At another time, Senator Jesse Helms, whom I believe to be a member of the Conspiracy's leadership, went on national television with an implied threat to President Clinton's life. He warned Clinton not to travel to a major United States Army base in North Carolina, Senator Helms's home state, because harm might come to him. Any such threat to a United States president, direct or implied, violates federal law. Yet there was precious little outcry in the media over Helms's illegal act. The Senate, which should have censured him, did nothing.

President Clinton responded. Doubtlessly aware of the documented dereliction of President Kennedy's virtually all-white, overwhelmingly WASP, Secret Service detail on that fateful day in Dallas, he took precautions against a repeat of such misbehavior. His personal Secret Service unit was overwhelmingly Black and had a Black commander. Clinton *knew* he could trust them.[3]

The attempted impeachment of President Bill Clinton was the sixth coup and failed miserably. While ostensibly focusing on trivial charges, the Conspiracy's aim was to overthrow a Democratic president who had attracted strong Black support, in order to replace him with its own Republican president who would cater openly to the new Confederacy. The Conspiracy's leading representatives at that time were Tom DeLay of Texas, deputy of the Speaker of the House of Representatives, and Trent Lott of Mississippi as Senate majority leader. When Trent Lott was forced to resign, he was replaced by Bill Frist of Tennessee.

The seventh coup perpetrated by the Conspiracy has been the most successful one. It legitimately installed its own hand-picked candidate as president (and would-be "emperor") of the United States. I refer to George Bush Jr.'s highjacking of the November 2000 presidential election with the open connivance of his brother, Florida Governor Jeb Bush, and the right-wing United States Supreme Court majority installed by their father, George H. W. Bush. What startled me was the extraordinary degree to which the robbed candidate, the mass media, the nation's bipartisan political and civic leadership, and the majority of the white public ignored the manifest illegitimacy of this brazen theft. Most Blacks openly called this coup by its right name.

I was reminded of the eerily similar contrast between the responses of white and Black Americans to the assassination of President John F. Kennedy thirty-seven years earlier. Then, as now, the same white leadership, media, and public swallowed whole the Warren Commission's fiction about "a single assassin," whereas most Blacks did not believe it. We are well aware from bitter experience that, in the main, white Americans are both unwilling and unable to face the obvious fact that their cherished image of America as the benevolent and wise "superpower" dispensing freedom, peace, and plenty around the world is in tatters abroad and in question among many at home.

The eighth coup was Bush's fraudulent victory in the 2004 presidential election. The Appendix to this book analyzes this unprecedented vote theft.

It should be evident that the top leadership of the Conspiracy is predominantly Southern. Moreover, it is permeated with fundamentalist Protestant ideology. Witness the open attempts by Tom DeLay and Attorney General John Ashcroft to violate the constitutionally mandated separation of church and state.

An acute danger is presented by President George W. Bush's open behavior in office as a religious zealot—a fundamentalist, born-again Christian who is bent on imposing his narrowminded, intolerant worldview on the entire human race. He has consistently implied his endorsement of the racist and anti-Semitic "Christian Nation" slogan of the Christian right, actively courting its organizations and leaders. His systematic increase of both the presence and power of fundamentalist Protestant religion throughout the federal government, coupled with the "faith-based initiative" he has inserted into civil society as a federally funded program, amounts to a subversion of the United States Constitution.

Bush is illegally forging a "Christian Nation," complete with its jingoistic and racist symbols. His "God and Country" superpatriotic rhetoric, his lily-white personal Secret Service detail, his open tolerance of the Confederate battle flag, his contempt for the multicolored United Nations, with its African secretary-general, his enmity toward openly secular European leaders, such as France's Jacques Chirac and Germany's Gerhard Schroeder, and his close friendship with British Prime Minister Tony Blair, a fellow born-again Christian, are all of one piece.

So we enter the twenty-first century with federal power usurped by an ignorant and partisan former governor of a formerly Confederate state. George W. Bush has revealed himself to be an arrogant, mean-spirited, venal fanatic who is hell-bent on establishing an imperial presidency. As the leader of "the world's only superpower," his publicly stated goal is to preside over "a new world order" through military threats. His openly imperialist rhetoric panders to the traditional enemies of African-Americans—the superpatriots who invariably are at the core of America's racist constituency and who believe fervently that God made them a superior nation and a superior race.

This monumental tragedy that has befallen the United States is not without an element of farce. For who could have imagined that a second-rate politician with the narrowest of visions and no acting ability could successfully parade for over four years as a powerful president and an influential world leader? In fact, he is a politically naked emperor. It is as if a scraggly East Texas shrub were to be displayed proudly as a California Redwood tree. However, in the harsh world of reality, Black Americans cannot afford to laugh at this political circus of the absurd. Nor can we afford to give way to cynicism or apathy. We must remember that a primary rule of politics is to punish one's enemies. The Republican Party, as a party, is our political enemy because it has been captured by its right-wing, Southern, Anglo-Saxon, fundamentalist-Protestant constituency. Our aim should be to crush it nationwide.

■ ■ ■

The tragedy of 9/11/01 could arguably have been prevented by adequate presidential leadership. The abject failure of the executive branch in assembling the available intelligence "dots" and connecting them has been investigated by an independent commission headed by former Republican Governor Thomas Keane of New Jersey. This commission was forced to overcome persistent attempts by the Bush administration to impede its work, but it exposed a mountain of evidence substantiating the view that the tragedy of 9/11 could have been prevented.

On September 18, 2002, Eleanor Hill, staff director of an inquiry into the 9/11 attacks, testified as follows before a joint Congressional Committee:

> Despite D.C.I.'s [Director of Central Intelligence] declaration of war in 1998, there was no massive shift in budget or reassignment of personnel to counter-terrorism until after Sept. 11, 2001. . . .

... In August 1998, the intelligence community obtained information that a group of unidentified Arabs planned to fly an explosive-laden airplane from a foreign country into the World Trade Center. The information was passed to the F.B.I. and the F.A.A. [Federal Aviation Authority]. ...

... In September 1998, the intelligence community obtained information that bin Laden's next operation would possibly involve flying an aircraft loaded with explosives into a U.S. airport and detonating it. This information was provided to senior U.S. government officials in late 1998. ...

Two days earlier, Condoleezza Rice, President Bush's National Security Adviser, who was one of the "senior government officials" who knew about this information, said that it had been "general" and had only "pointed toward potential attacks overseas." She added: "I don't think anyone could have predicted that these people would take an airplane and slam it into the World Trade Center, take another one and slam it into the Pentagon, that they would try to use an airplane as a missile."

These statements were demonstrably untrue.

A June 19, 2002, story in the *New York Times* provides a detailed description of how Phoenix, Arizona, FBI Agent Kenneth Williams, a terrorism expert, had been tracking suspected Al Qaeda members who were training at Arizona flight schools. His superiors shelved his reports. According to FBI Director Robert Mueller, they did so because the reports lacked "specificity."

Since the 1993 World Trade Center bombing, the CIA and FBI had been aware of the threat of airplanes being used as weapons to ram buildings. The CIA warned in 1999 that terrorists might hijack a plane and use it as a missile to strike the White House, the Pentagon, or CIA headquarters. In the summer of 2001, Italian intelligence sources warned of the possibility that Al Qaeda might try to hijack a plane and slam it into the Genoa summit headquarters.

This combined advance knowledge, or even any significant part of it, was certainly sufficient to have prevented the 9/11 tragedy. The very possibility of this disaster could have been eliminated by spending the money required to make the hijacking of planes virtually impossible. Israel, a far smaller, more vulnerable, and less affluent country, has been able to achieve this. A second highly reliable defense would have been to expend the funds required to establish the nationwide capability to locate, intercept, and if necessary demolish in the air any hijacked plane before it could reach a target of World Trade Center magnitude.

Ms. Rice also voiced the disingenuous complaints that the intelligence reports were "general," that the intelligence organizations had not shared information with one another, and that no one had "connected the dots." By their nature, intelligence reports are rarely specific. They are usually both general and speculative. And although the FBI and the CIA may not have shared information with each other, they had both sent their information to Ms. Rice, who at the time was both the president's National Security Adviser and chairperson of the National Security Council. As such, it was her responsibility to connect the intelligence dots. Not only was 9/11 preventable, but Condoleezza Rice's personal failure to prevent 9/11 dwarfs everyone else's, with one exception.

President Bush was briefed on August 6, 2001, about Osama bin Laden's plan to carry out airline hijackings in the United States, but he took no action. Apparently, he was more concerned about getting Congress to finance his antimissile defense scheme. This disclosure, which came eight months after the 9/11 attacks, outraged some of the victims' families. A few even speculated out loud as to whether President Bush had permitted the disaster to happen, "knowing the wave of national unity" that would follow. A timid collection of congressional Democrats ran like rabbits from questions of this kind, while the President fiercely resisted the formation of an independent commission to investigate 9/11. A year would pass until he reluctantly agreed to the panel's formation, and another year would elapse before he finally began to release the documents it requested.

Four wives of 9/11 victims had no confidence in the administration's statements. Suspecting a cover-up, they launched their own investigation which revealed the following:[4]

■ The FBI told them that it didn't investigate flight schools before 9/11 because of the prohibitively large number of such schools. Yet a few hours after the 9/11 attacks, FBI agents showed up at the Embry-Riddle flight school in Florida where several of the terrorists had trained.

■ An FBI agent denied that prior to 9/11 the Bureau had any open investigations of the terrorists responsible for the attacks. On July 24, 2003, it was publicly revealed in a briefing by Eleanor Hill, staff director of the congressional inquiry into the 9/11 attacks, that the FBI had fourteen open investigations of persons who had contact with the hijackers while they were in the United States.

■ A video was found showing President Bush's reaction fourteen minutes after the first plane crashed into the World Trade Center on the morning of September 11. He was told of the attack in the hallway of a Washington, D.C., elementary school. He went to a private room, spoke by phone with his National Security Adviser, Condoleezza Rice, and looked at a TV in the room. "That's some bad pilot," he said. Then he went to a classroom to read to second graders. He remained there even after an aide whispered into his ear that a second plane had struck the towers and that the United States was under attack.

■ The Federal Aviation Authority and the Secret Service both knew at 8:20 a.m. on 9/11 that two planes had been hijacked in the New York area. By 8:43 a.m., the FAA had identified them as Flights Nos. 11 and 175 and notified the North American Aerospace Defense Command. By 9:02 a.m., both planes had crashed into the World Trade Center. However, neither the North American Aerospace Defense Command nor the FAA took any action, even though they knew there were two other hijacked planes in the air.

■ Secretary of Defense Donald Rumsfeld was busy with his regular intelligence briefing in his Washington office. After he had been informed of the two attacks on the World Trade Center, he continued with his briefing until the Pentagon was struck by a third hijacked plane.

The four wives, having lost their trust in the credibility of the Bush administration, raised a series of searching questions: Why did President Bush dismiss the attack on the first tower as an accident by a "bad pilot"? Why did he stay in a second-grade classroom after being informed that the United States was under attack? Why did Secretary of Defense Rumsfeld continue with his regular briefing after being informed of the two attacks on the World Trade Center? And why did both the Federal Aviation Authority and the North

American Aerospace Defense Command fail to issue any warning during the forty minutes that elapsed between their discovery of the hijackings and the first attack?

Some relatives of 9/11 victims have openly speculated that the Bush administration deliberately permitted the terrorist attacks to succeed in order to exploit the anger and grief of the American people in the service of the President's foreign and domestic agendas. They are not alone. A number of intrepid reporters have uncovered and published a significant body of evidence pointing in this direction. And many Blacks, to a far greater extent than most whites, are open to considering this possibility.

Having reconstituted itself as a private investigative body, I hope that the former independent commission for the investigation of 9/11 will address this question explicitly.

■ ■ ■

President Bush's résumé is pitifully inadequate for an aspiring United States president and an embarrassment for a would-be world emperor.

Accepted by Yale University despite his mediocre high-school record, his major college distinction was to make the cheerleader squad. He avoided combat duty in Vietnam by joining the Texas Air National Guard, and was not punished for going AWOL.

In 1976 he had a serious brush with the law in Kennebunkport, Maine. Arrested for driving under the influence of alcohol, he pled guilty, paid a fine, and had his driver's license suspended for thirty days. His Texas driving record has been lost and is not available. With regard to his alleged cocaine use, he refused to take a drug test and has consistently refused to answer any questions.

His work experience is unimpressive. He ran for United States Congress and lost. He bought a Texas oil company, couldn't find any oil, and sold all his stock just before he declared bankruptcy. Then he bought the Texas baseball team in a questionable deal that appropriated land using taxpayer money. He was elected governor of Texas with the help of George H.W. Bush's friends, including the subsequently convicted Enron CEO, Ken Lay.

At the end of George Bush's term as Governor, Texas was the most polluted state in the union; Houston was the most smog-ridden city in America; the Texas treasury was bankrupted because of his tax cuts; and he had set the record for the most executions ever carried out in one state.

As president, Bush has degraded the security of the United States to its lowest ebb in modern history. His domestic policies have left our economy in shambles and our foreign policy in bankruptcy.

Within his first two years in office, Bush spent the large United States budget surplus accumulated during the eight years of the Clinton administration, effectively bankrupting the United States Treasury. Simultaneously, he presided over the biggest drop in the history of the United States stock market and created the largest annual deficit in American history.

During his first year as president, over two million Americans lost their jobs, and this trend continued for the next two years. In 2003, he presided over the biggest energy crisis in our nation's history and refused to intervene when corruption was revealed in the oil industry. His largest lifetime contributor, Kenneth Lay, was convicted for the most extensive corporate bankruptcy fraud ever perpetrated: the

"Enron scandal." Yet he protected Lay and other such corporate criminals against Federal prosecution.

The Bush foreign policy has sharply reduced America's security and has resulted in an unprecedented degree of United States isolation from its closest allies. More than two-thirds of all Europeans view the Bush presidency as the greatest threat to world peace and security. Their fears have been confirmed by Bush's support of a nuclear Tactical Bunker Buster for use in a worldwide War Against Terror, in contravention of the Geneva Convention and the United Nations Charter.

In addition, Bush has broken more international treaties than any other United States president and has withdrawn the United States from the World Court of Law. He has refused to sign both the Kyoto Agreement on global warming and the Human Rights Convention.[5]

Several years ago, Nelson Mandela, former President of South Africa, sharply criticized President George W. Bush's America. He said: "One power, with a president who has no foresight and cannot think properly, is now wanting to plunge the world into a holocaust."

With such a dismal record before and after a highly controversial ascent to the White House, how is it that President George W. Bush has been successful in temporarily convincing a decisive segment of the United States electorate that he is a trustworthy, strong, albeit flawed, leader? How has he been able to sell demonstrably wrong and failed domestic and foreign policies to at least half of the American public? Why has no coherent political opposition to these policies yet emerged? And why, given the already disastrous consequences of Bush's failed initiatives, is there no popular revolt against him?

Bush is certainly ignorant, but he is not stupid. As one of the most skillful politicians in recent memory, he has converted his character flaws into assets. His crude arrogance plays well to a right-wing Anglo-Saxon constituency, especially when it is wrapped in the traditional code words of an Anglo-Saxon, Christian crusade for world domination. In the February 24, 2003, issue of the *New York Observer*, columnist Nicholas Von Hoffman wrote:

> Assumptions of the inferiority of the Muslim religion and Arabic civilization suffuse every statement coming out of Washington, where the Anglo-Saxon chieftains are poised to let loose a firestorm on the inhabitants of the region of the Tigris and Euphrates rivers. The threat of a religio-cultural, imperial war of domination has terrified the Middle East. The officialdom in those parts is suffering premonitions about what happens after Iraq is destroyed. The Anglo-Saxons haven't exactly been discreet about their intentions: Saudi Arabia is next as, one by one, the U.S. lops off the present heads of state, installs its own puppets and calls it democracy.

However, there is another America that is not a part of Bush's right-wing constituency. It is the America that won the war for civil rights, opposed the Vietnam War, and now opposes Bush's foreign and domestic policies. This is the America that African-Americans have traditionally supported and support now. It is not Bush's America.

We Blacks know our right-wing Anglo-Saxon enemies well. For generations, they have oppressed us—first as slaves, then as second-class citizens. In the past we were taught to fear them because we were alone. Now, we no longer fear them and are no longer alone. Moreover, their constituency has shrunk to less than half the total United States population, and their unity is beginning to unravel.

Blacks' greatest contribution to Bush's political defeat would be the exposure of his real cultural and political identity. We should demonstrate publicly at every opportunity that, as a united people, we oppose Bush's policies, his cultural values, and his core right-wing Anglo-Saxon constituency.

We should do so with intensity and consistency with the goal of compelling the white media to acknowledge our political hostility to the President. In the South, which provides the base of Bush's support, we should force sharp political polarization. In my view, Bush's Anglo-Saxon gang with its racist southern core constituency cannot govern a politically polarized nation.

NOTES

1. Robert Dallek, in an article published in the June, 2003, issue of the *Atlantic Monthly*, presents a thoroughly researched analysis of President John F. Kennedy's plans for his second term and his deep commitments to equal opportunity, an economic "safety net" for all Americans, and an end to the Cold War. Most Blacks liked and trusted Kennedy as a progressive president in the mold of Abraham Lincoln and Franklin D. Roosevelt. We also admired his personal elegance, grace, and subtlety, and identified with him as an "ethnic" Irish Catholic—the only non-WASP ever to be president of the United States.

2. *The Triumph of Politics*, by David A. Stockman, Harper and Row, New York, 1986.

3. The FBI, the CIA, and the Secret Service were not fully trusted by either Kennedy or Clinton. All of these agencies, as well as Military Intelligence, have generally been dominated by the right wing of the WASP establishment. J. Edgar Hoover, who served as FBI Director for forty years, beginning in 1927, was suspected of being one of the leaders of the WASP Conspiracy.

4. *New York Observer*, August 25–September 1, 2003.

5. The summary of Bush's record before and after he assumed the office of the presidency is based entirely on widely published original materials. I have adapted the version I obtained through a friend from the e-mail address—StuartEee@aol.com.

CHAPTER III

THE "WAR ON TERROR"

On November 15, 1989, Colin Powell, then Chairman of the Joint Chiefs of Staff, submitted a definitive strategy document to President George H. W. Bush proposing that the United States set out to achieve world dominance. Three years later, Powell told Congress that, "the United States requires sufficient power . . . to deter any challenger from ever dreaming of challenging us on the world stage. . . . I want to be the bully on the block." Since then, the steady rise in terrorist attacks against the United States and its allies, including the 9/11 outrage, has been a response to the pursuit of this policy.

Most Blacks oppose both the Bush Doctrine and all of the policies deriving from it. Experience has taught us that such a militaristic foreign policy invariably appeals to the racist and corporate constituencies at home and to right-wing constituencies abroad. It always undermines our vital economic interests by diverting huge expenditures of public funds away from the social spending that is a prerequisite for any significant Black economic advancement. It also runs counter to our cultural and religious traditions of opposing all military actions except defensive ones.

President George W. Bush's "preemptive war" doctrine, proclaimed in 2002 and marketed by then National Security

Adviser Condoleezza Rice, was an unabashed announcement of the current Bush administration's intention to pursue world domination through military power. Its public unveiling in the wake of the 9/11 terrorist attack served as background for President Bush's opportunistic exploitation of New York City's martyrdom to advance his militaristic agenda.

Instead of building an effective international counterterrorist campaign while installing an effective home security system, Bush launched the metaphorical War Against Terror to frighten the American people into the acceptance of his unilateralist foreign policy in the name of "self-defense." Having achieved this goal, he invaded two countries while neglecting the completion of even a stop-gap home security system.

The wars against Afghanistan and Iraq are designed to control the oil resources of Central Asia and the Middle East, respectively, rather than to isolate and root out terrorists.[1] By now it is clear to all but the most obtuse that these wars require prolonged occupation, regime change to a government that is certain to be totally subservient to the United States, and large permanent United States military bases on the territory of Iraq and Afghanistan.

The declared goal of "bringing democracy and a better life" to Iraq and Afghanistan is a flat lie—a lie that Blacks recognize as such because of our memory of the Mexican and Phillipine wars; the overt and covert interventions in Cuba, Haiti, China, Korea, Iran, Ghana, the Belgian Congo, Vietnam, Laos, and Cambodia; Guatemala, Chile, Nicaragua, and Colombia; Grenada and Panama. Most of these military and paramilitary interventions were aimed at colonizing the people of the Third World in the interests of the "globalization" program of the United States corporate establishment.

The price of this deception is high. The methods required to combat terrorism are antithetical to those required to wage conventional wars. Experience has demonstrated that conventional wars tend to produce, rather than to combat, terrorism. No wonder that the War against Terror has failed to make America safer from real-life terrorists. Moreover, the national debate about the continuing wars in Afghanistan and Iraq is unfolding in the absence of an effective United States counterterrorism capability.

It is well known that fifteen of the nineteen hijacker terrorists who perpetrated the 9/11 atrocity came from Saudi Arabia and that the Saudis remain the chief source of Al Qaeda funding. Yet the White House continues to maintain its close ties with the leaders of the Saudi royal family. Bush's cover-up of the Saudi connection to 9/11 is part of a wider cover-up of the Bush administration's abject failure to protect the nation from the 9/11 terrorist attack. The report of the 9/11 Commission reveals that both President Bush and National Security Adviser Rice lied when they asserted after 9/11 that there had been no evidence that bin Laden planned to attack in the United States, that using planes as missiles had been impossible to predict, that the FBI and CIA could not have foreseen 9/11, and that neither the airlines nor the United States military establishment could have imagined 9/11.[2]

The war against Afghanistan's Taliban rulers, officially aimed at capturing or killing the perpetrators of the 9/11 attack, was actually a war for the purpose of regime change. Osama bin Laden and his Al Qaeda accomplices have found relatively safe haven in the border regions of western Pakistan, along with the Taliban leadership. From these bases, they are successfully destabilizing eastern Afghanistan and continue to undermine the stability of Pakistan, which is our closest ally in the region. A continuation of Bush's policy will cause United States troops to be mired in Afghanistan for years in a war of occupation with no hope of victory.

The second war, the long-planned attack against Saddam Hussein, was launched behind a screen of subterfuge and without adequate preparation. Now, over two years after the fall of Baghdad, no trace of weapons of mass destruction or of a viable program to produce them has been found in Iraq. Since Saddam's access to weapons of mass destruction was the primary reason given for the invasion, the Iraq war is both unwarranted and illegal under international law. Furthermore, the successful campaign to overthrow Saddam Hussein has degenerated into a second war of occupation, resisted by both a growing section of the Iraqi people and a vocal minority of the American people.

The Bush administration's foreign policy has made the American people and people in many other countries around the world less safe, has proliferated terrorists, has isolated the United States internationally, and has united large parts of the world in active opposition to the United States. Its prohibitive cost has undermined the nation's economy and, by March 2006, resulted in official United States military casualties amounting to 2,300 dead and 15,000 wounded, with no end in sight.

Worse still, the Bush administration remains in denial of a mountain of evidence confirming that rising Islamic terrorism is a response to United States foreign policy in general and the Iraq war in particular. A July 19, 2005, article in the *New York Times* reported that the British Joint Terrorism Analysis Centre concluded in mid-June 2005 that "events in Iraq are continuing to act as motivation and a focus of a range of terrorist related activity in the U.K."

■ ■ ■

President Bush has fostered a policy of unlimited foreign military intervention in pursuit of regime changes ever since his first inauguration. Our nation has suffered such misanthropic presidents in the past. It is said that Karl Rove, the architect of President Bush's political strategy, is a great admirer of President William McKinley, who acquired an overseas empire in order to "civilize" and "Christianize" the peoples of the Spanish colonies. We should recall that an easy military victory over Spain in the Philippine Islands was followed by a protracted and brutal United States war of pacification against the Philippine people, which slaughtered hundreds of thousands of civilians.

Theodore Roosevelt, one of Bush's main heroes, wrote the following to a friend four years before he was inaugurated as president: "In strict confidence . . . I should welcome almost any war, for I think this country needs one."[3] When he became president, he revealed himself to be a messianic imperialist and a confirmed racist who condoned lynching and believed he belonged to a master race. In his essay "Greetings from the Nineteenth to the Twentieth Century," Mark Twain satirized imperial America: "I bring you the stately nation named Christendom, returning bedraggled, besmirched, dishonored, from pirate raids into Kiao-Chu, Manchuria, South Africa and the Philippines, with her soul full of meanness, her pocket full of boodle, and her mouth full of pious hypocrisies. Give her soap and a towel, but hide the looking glass."[4]

General Dwight D. Eisenhower responded as follows when he was presented with a proposal for preemptive war in 1956: "In this day and time . . . I don't believe there is such a thing; and, frankly, I wouldn't even listen to anyone seriously that came in and talked about it."[5]

It is against this background that we should view an August 2001 report commissioned by Secretary of Defense Donald Rumsfeld that presents the Roman and Chinese empires as the models for a new world order imposed by United States military force. Bush's constant pronouncements in his speeches during October and November 2001 were aimed at preparing the American people for multiple wars against nations whose regimes he wanted to change, rather than against terrorists:

> Each nation comes with a different set of capabilities and a different willingness to help. America says, "We don't care how you help, just help. Either you're for us or against us. If you house a terrorist, you're just as guilty as the terrorists themselves." . . . This is our nation's time to lead the world, and we're going to do that. . . . We will not waver.
>
> The United States is presenting a clear choice to every nation: Stand with the civilized world, or stand with the terrorists. And for those nations that stand with the terrorists, there will be a heavy price.[6]

Many well-meaning whites believed President Bush because they trusted him. Most Blacks do not trust him and are not inclined to believe anything he says. In the case of his remarks above, we recognized them for the arrogant bluster they resembled. We also braced for the disastrous consequences we saw coming.

The September 20, 2002, issue of the *New York Times* carried a major piece about President Bush's new foreign policy doctrine, "The National Security Strategy of the United

States," as presented by one of its chief architects, National Security Adviser Condoleezza Rice. The substance and tone of this official document echoed the Pentagon's review submitted three months earlier.

It claimed the "right of self-defense by acting preemptively against . . . terrorists. . . . We must deter and defend against the threat before it is unleashed." Elsewhere it contained a not-so-veiled military threat against Russia and China: "Our forces will be strong enough to dissuade potential adversaries from pursuing a military buildup in the hopes of surpassing, or equaling, the power of the United States." This threat was underscored by a reaffirmation of Bush's decision to abandon the Anti-Ballistic Missile Treaty because it impeded United States efforts to build a missile defense system. The thirty-three-page document also stated bluntly that "The president has no intention of allowing any foreign power to catch up with the huge [military] lead the United States has opened up since the fall of the Soviet Union."

The same issue of the *New York Times* carried an article about the response to a remark made by German Justice Minister Herta Daeubler-Gmelin about United States President George W. Bush. She had sharply criticized his militaristic, superpatriotic rhetoric, adding that "Bush wants to divert attention from his domestic problems. It's a classic tactic. It's one that Hitler also used." Her reply to official U.S. outrage over her comment was unapologetic: "I didn't compare the persons Bush and Hitler, but their methods." In my view, she could have added that there is some similarity between the imperialistic foreign policies of Hitler's Germany and Bush's America.

■ ■ ■

By mid-September of 2002, United States Secretary of State Colin Powell had convinced President Bush to seek the collaboration of the United Nations and to reject the advice of Secretary of Defense Donald Rumsfeld and his coterie of Pentagon hawks. Bush's decision was signaled by his op-ed piece in the September 11, 2002, issue of the *New York Times*. It was titled, "Securing Freedom's Triumph" and elaborated on the theme that "America's greatest opportunity is to create a balance of world power that favors human freedom."

However, the next two sentences belied the relatively restrained tone of all that followed:

> We will use our position of unparalleled strength and influence to build an atmosphere of international order and openness in which progress and liberty can flourish in many nations. A peaceful world of growing freedom serves American long-term interests, reflects American ideals and unites America's allies.

Rumsfeld's nuclear fist shows through Bush's velvet glove. When President Bush stated publicly that, if the United Nations did not act, the United States would unilaterally ensure that there were no weapons of mass destruction in Iraq, he alienated both United Nations Secretary-General Kofi Annan and a majority of UN Security Council members. As a result, the occupations of both Iraq and Afghanistan remain primarily United States operations.

After more than two years of the occupation of Iraq by coalition military forces, no trace of ties between Saddam Hussein's regime and Al Qaeda has been discovered. Less than a month after Bush's remarks, Czech President Vaclav Havel publicly discredited reports that Mohammad Atta, the operational leader of the 9/11 terrorist hijackings, had met with an Iraqi intelligence officer in Prague in April of 2001. George J. Tenet, Director of the CIA, told Congress in mid-October of 2002 that the CIA had no evidence that such a meeting had occurred. Czech officials declared that they had no evidence that Mohammad Atta was even in the country in April of 2001, and United States records indicate that he was in Virginia Beach, Va. earlier that month.

After many months of effort by thousands of trained personnel, no chemical, biological, or nuclear weapons have been discovered in Iraq, despite the investment of $1.5 billion in a nationwide search. No evidence of materials, equipment, or programs required to produce weapons of mass destruction has been found. On the contrary, the evidence discovered substantiates the view that, long before the United States invasion, the Iraqi regime had terminated all programs and dispersed all personnel groups that might be capable of reconstituting a viable program for producing weapons of mass destruction.

Most likely, all weapons, materials, and equipment that could possibly be associated with even a potential capability to use weapons of mass destruction were destroyed by the Iraqi regime after the 1991 Gulf War. The search has been quietly abandoned.

■ ■ ■

Far from "securing and reconstructing" Iraq, "our coalition" has suffered more casualties in the occupation than in the war and is engaged in a counterinsurgency war reminiscent of Vietnam. The Iraqi infrastructure remains in shambles, and $13 billion in aid pledges from the United States and other countries has evaporated into a paltry $630 million in actual contributions. The $87 billion aid "for Iraq" that the Bush administration rammed through Congress will go almost entirely to finance the coalition occupation forces. Very little, if anything, will go directly to the Iraqi people. Virtually all of the money earmarked for "the reconstruction of Iraq" has been funneled through lucrative "no-bid" contracts awarded to United States corporations run by President Bush's cronies. A prime example of the corruption pervading this process has surfaced in the form of the scandal surrounding the contracts awarded to the Halliburton Company, in which Vice President Cheney maintains an interest.

This tawdry affair serves as a reminder that the real goal of the Bush Administration is to restore the Iraqi revenue-producing infrastructure for America's benefit. No wonder a majority of the Iraqi people have come to distrust and oppose the United States occupation. Only a radical policy change—one that guarantees that all funding for the rebuilding of Iraq is delivered directly to the Iraqi Government—can begin to change this justified Iraqi skepticism. By now it appears that a United States "victory" in the Iraq war is impossible without such a change.

Since Bush's unilateralism has alienated him from America's main European allies and from the United Nations, there is no prospect of significant aid to Iraq from United States allies unless President Bush relinquishes both political and military control of Iraq's occupation to the United Nations Security Council. And unless a democratic constitution for Iraq is adopted by the end of 2006, the United States will be compelled to begin a negotiated withdrawal from Iraq. Otherwise, an unwinnable Vietnam-like "quagmire," unacceptable to at least two-thirds of United States voters, will become an unavoidable certainty.

In the face of a steadily intensifying insurgency that is gaining strength and has driven Iraq to the brink of civil war, the possibility that a constitution can be adopted by January 1, 2007 is vanishing. Therefore, common sense dictates that the Bush administration should begin immediate negotiations with the Iraqi interim government to withdraw from Iraq unconditionally by January 1, 2007.

Such an initiative would greatly strengthen the authority of that temporary body. It would also provide the Iraqis themselves with a realistic opportunity to avoid a civil war and to hold nationwide democratic elections. Most important of all, it would certainly isolate the insurgency politically and probably weaken it fatally in the military sense.[7]

However, a so-called "exit strategy," which is rapidly becoming ever more difficult to execute successfully, is officially not even in the discussion stage. The only statements emanating from the Bush administration on this matter are the twin mantras: "We will prevail" and "We will stay the course."

Meanwhile, the results of Bush's wars have been uniformly disastrous and are becoming intolerable. The wars in Iraq and Afghanistan have failed to produce stable democratic regimes. The official casualty figures released by the Department of Defense are grossly underreported, and no official figures have been released for Iraqi and Afghan civilian casualties.

Red Crescent, International Red Cross, and United Nations estimates of Iraqi civilian casualties since the beginning of the war over two years ago range as high as 100,000. According to the unreleased Department of Defense casualty lists, United States military deaths from all causes have reached a total of over 6,000, and the number of wounded or injured from all causes is over 24,000. In addition, over 5,000 have deserted.

It appears to me that the American people will not permit this war to continue beyond another year. This probability has been increased by the recent release of the Downing Street Memo by the British government.

In the memo, the Director of the British Foreign Intelligence Service (MI-6) confirms that in July of 2002, at a time when President Bush was assuring the United States public and the Congress that no decision had been made on whether to go to war against Iraq, Bush had already decided to go to war to remove Saddam Hussein. The memo added that "the intelligence and facts were being fixed around the policy." British Foreign Secretary Jack Straw later commented that "The case was thin. Saddam was not threatening his neighbors, and his WMD capability was less than that of Libya, North Korea or Iran." Now the entire world knows that President Bush lied in order to plunge America into an unjustified and illegal war.

The severely weakened "coalition of the willing" which now occupies Iraq is rapidly disintegrating, with many of the coalition members already committed to the withdrawal of their personnel by the end of 2006. If and when the transitional Iraqi government agrees on a constitution and gets it ratified by the Iraqi people, the permanent government elected under the constitution is likely to request that United States troops leave within at most a year. Since even this bleak outcome is, in present circumstances, overly optimistic, it has become obvious to virtually all impartial observers that current United States policy in both Iraq and Afghanistan has failed hopelessly.

During the latter part of July 2005, the Bush administration quietly jettisoned the metaphorical War On Terror, replacing it with the realistic phrase, "global struggle against violent extremism." The "war" has become a struggle, and the "terrorists" have become violent extremists.

On July 23, 2005, two top White House officials published an op-ed piece in the *New York Times* calling this struggle "an ideological contest, a war of ideas." According to *U.S. News and World Report*, a new Pentagon strategy document calls the threat faced by the United States "Islamist extremism . . . that exploits Islam for political ends." In June 2005, Wallace Gregson, a Marine lieutenant general, said in a speech that "This is no more a war on terrorism than the Second World War was a war on submarines. . . . The decisive terrain in this war is the vast majority of people who are not directly involved." On July 12, 2005, Secretary of Defense Donald Rumsfeld used the new language, repeating the word "extremist" or variations of it eleven times at a press conference.

However, on August 3, 2005, President Bush used the occasion of his speech delivered in Grapevine, Texas, to assert bluntly: "Make no mistake about it, we are at war." He proceeded to use the word "war" thirteen times in referring to the terrorist threat in a speech ostensibly devoted to his domestic policies. Two days earlier, on August 1, Secretary of Defense Donald Rumsfeld had emphatically backed away from his previous new language:

> Some ask, "are we still engaged in a war on terror?" Let there be no mistake about it. It's a war. The president properly termed it that after September 11. The only way to defend against terrorism is to go on the attack.

However, the decisive word on this matter was enunciated by General Richard B. Myers of the Air Force, Chairman of the Joint Chiefs of Staff, who spoke on behalf of the United States military command on July 18. In an address to the National Press Club, he said bluntly that he had "objected to the use of the term 'war on terrorism' before, because if you call it a war, then you think of people in uniform being the solution." General Myers then added that the threat instead should be defined as violent extremists with the recognition that "terror is the method they use."[8]

General Myers completely contradicted all of President Bush's repeated formulations on this central issue, including every possible interpretation of them. He did so in a prime national public forum and has so far demonstrated no inclination to retract any portion of his comprehensive refutation of his commander-in-chief's position. Moreover, in direct contradiction to Bush's policy of indefinite military status quo in Iraq, General George W. Casey, the top United States military commander in Iraq, has publicly announced the need to begin reducing United States troop strength in Iraq "substantially" as early as March 2006.

These developments are proof that the top command of the United States military establishment is actively engaged in publicly contradicting and practically undermining President Bush's entire military policy, including his phony War On Terror. This military insubordination serves as a stark reminder of the complete bankruptcy of the Bush Doctrine. It alone is sufficient grounds for suspecting that this president and his cabinet are bent on capturing unbridled political power "by any means necessary."

NOTES

1. See President George W. Bush's public remarks, September 11–26, 2003, *"We Will Prevail," President George W. Bush On War, Terrorism, and Freedom*, A National Review Book, New York–London, Continuum Publishing Group, 2003.

2. U.S. President Theodore Roosevelt letter to a friend in 1897.

3. Twain, Mark. "A Salutation from the 19th to the 20th Century," *Twain: Collected Tales, Sketches, Speeches, and Essays : Volume 2: 1891–1910* , Library of America, October 15, 1992.

4. Bob Fitrakis and Harvey Wasserman, "Bush and America's Willing Executioners would be Guilty at Nuremberg," *The Free Press,* March 2, 2003.

5. *The 9/11 Commission Report*, New York, W. W. Norton & Company, 2004; Paul Thompson and the Center for Cooperative Research, *The Terror Timeline*, New York, Regan Books, 2004.

6. Presidential speech at the Department of Labor, October 4, 2001, and Presidential radio address to the nation, October 6, 2001.

7. *New York Times*, October 6, 2003.

8. From an article by George Packer in the August 8 and 15 issue of *The New Yorker*, August 8–15, 2005; the *New York Times*, August 4, 2005.

CHAPTER IV

ECONOMICS, RACE, AND CLASS

Black Americans are a cohesive ethnic group with a distinct culture defined by historical experience. Our common bonds have been forged in the successive trials of slavery, enforced segregation, institutional racism, and the continued denial of equal opportunity.

From this vantage point, the majority of us perceive our economic interests to be substantially different from those of mainstream America. For example, we reject the idea that a free-market, supply-side, deregulated economy is the best system. We favor a mixed-market, producer-side, regulated system modeled after Franklin D. Roosevelt's New Deal economy and based on the principles established by Alexander Hamilton, Benjamin Franklin, and Abraham Lincoln. We support the expansion of the public sector, tax increases on annual family incomes above $100,000, fair trade instead of free trade, and protection of domestic markets and jobs in place of globalization and outsourcing. And we strongly oppose privatization of any portion of the public sector, including social security. Debt increases and tax cuts are viewed as contrary to our economic interests.

The reasons for these attitudes are rooted in our cultural traditions and in our American experience. Our culture puts a high value on an honest day's work; professionals command a higher prestige than entrepreneurs; obtaining a good education has a higher priority than the mere acquisition of wealth, and people are valued above property. The collective well-being is considered more important than the advancement of the individual.

Although it is true that since the passage of the Civil Rights Act and the Voting Rights Act the new African-American entrepreneurial middle class has in large part abandoned these priorities and adopted the ethos of the mainstream culture, the Black working-class majority has retained the core of the old cultural traditions.

The civil rights *movement* ended when its goal was met by the landmark congressional passage of the Civil Rights Act of 1965 and its signing by President Lyndon Johnson. The new goal put forward by the right wing of the civil rights leadership—the leaders of the NAACP and the Urban League—was the narrow one of seeking full equal opportunity in employment under the new laws. The strategy of nonviolent mass action was abandoned in favor of massive voter registration, legislative lobbying, and economic self-help. Its main political allies were the right wing of the Democratic Party and the right wing of the AFL-CIO leadership.

Rev. Martin Luther King, Jr., chose a different path based on nonviolent mass action and mass voter registration for the purpose of compelling the federal government to enforce immediate equal opportunity for all minorities throughout both the public and private sectors of the economy. He chose the left wing of the Democratic Party and the left wing of the AFL-CIO as his main political allies.

A majority of the Black middle class, especially the older generation, sided with the right wing of the civil rights leadership. A minority, including the left wing of the civil rights

leadership, supported King. A majority of the Black working class and poor supported King. A minority supported
the rising Black Power movement, whose radical objective
was the achievement of full economic and social equality
through the direct application of independent Black political power. The strategy of the movement entailed the sever-
ing of alliances with white liberals and the full Black control
of Black communities.

The "cultural revolution" of the white middle class, the
"white backlash" against implementation of the civil rights
laws, and violent economic rebellions of the Black urban
poor appeared often in the headlines in the fifteen years
between the passage of civil rights legislation in 1965 and
Ronald Reagan's election to the presidency in 1980. The
drama of those times, coupled with the War on Poverty,
largely obscured the phenomenally rapid rise of the new,
largely entrepreneurial Black middle class and the continuous relative economic decline of the Black working class and
the Black poor.

Beginning in 1980, the twelve years of the Reagan and
George H. W. Bush conservative counterrevolution further
degraded the economic status of the entire United States
working-class and poor population, whereas the middle and
upper classes thrived. Affirmative action, with the goal of
advancing minorities through the achievement of diversity
in the work force and in academia was applied in such a way
as to advance the Black middle class without substantially
benefiting the Black working class and poor.

This policy, which pitted the Black middle class against
the working class, was implemented by severely limiting the
possibility of legally enforcing affirmative action. As a result,
affirmative-action policies complied with the guidelines set

by the corporate sector to meet their need for skilled minority employees to compensate for the rapidly growing shortage of white skilled labor. These would have the opportunity to rise into the middle class. The vast number of relatively unskilled minority workers were left without assistance.

The legal foundation for this affirmative-action system was laid by United States Supreme Court Justice Sandra Day O'Connor in her landmark majority opinion written in 1986 in a case involving quotas. Its carefully designed language meets employer specifications fully.

The heart of the court's ruling in the language of O'Connor's majority opinion was the flat declaration that "quotas" were illegal under the United States Constitution. It defined a quota as follows:

> a fixed number or percentage of persons of a particular race, color, religion, sex or national origin which must be attained . . . , regardless of whether such persons meet the necessary qualifications to perform the job.

This means that the term "quota" can legally be applied to mandatory results in minority hiring *only* if the persons are hired regardless of their qualifications.

If the hiring is restricted to persons who meet the qualifications for the job, then the hiring of "a fixed number or percentage" cannot be defined as a quota and is therefore legal. Quotas for qualified (that is, middle class) Blacks are legal. Quotas for unqualified (working class and poor) Blacks are illegal. Therefore, employers can discriminate at will against the latter group merely by claiming that they are "unqualified."

Justice O'Connor's opinion was a cynical manipulation of language and law to suit the requirements of an employer constituency. It makes a mockery of the fawning adulation heaped upon her when she announced that she intended to retire. It has also exposed the fundamental flaw in the policy of affirmative action by rendering it useless to a majority of Blacks.

This flaw resides in the Civil Rights Act itself. Its stated purpose is to rectify *past* discrimination instead of mandating the elimination of *present* discrimination.[1] The enforcement of a policy designed to right past wrongs is next to impossible to enforce in practice. On the other hand, a policy designed to end present discrimination is easily enforced if the will exists to do so. All that is required is a system of specific minimum quotas universally enforced by the federal government.

A specific minimum quota is a mandatory fixed number of positions reserved for a specific minority group. That number must be equal to a significant percentage (say 20 percent) of the equitable number that is commensurate with the relative size of the group. For example, if Blacks are 25 percent of the population, they would automatically be entitled to at least 5 percent employment everywhere. After that start, they would be on their own.

Such a program designed to eliminate institutional racism would include the private sector, academia, and the public sector, along with all government agencies such as the CIA, the FBI, the Department of State, the Department of Defense, the criminal justice system, and the United States Congress.

The issue of affirmative action has assumed such importance over the past forty years because it has been the only available weapon with which to combat workplace discrimination. Since it has proved to be woefully inadequate without an enforcement mechanism, the brand-new weapon of mandated equal opportunity must be enacted by Congress, with compliance measured by the *result*, rather than by mere intent.

The eight Clinton years, from 1992 to 2000, halted the downward economic slide of working class and poor, but the emphasis on debt reduction restricted social spending to a level that precluded any significant gains. At the same time, Clinton's engaging personality, populist image and unrivalled political skill headed off any revival of a much needed mass movement.

In the absence of such a movement, the economic and political status quo consolidated by Ronald Reagan and George H. W. Bush strengthened itself during the Clinton years. By 2000, the labor movement was at its weakest in seventy years, and the Black freedom movement had been dismantled and dispersed. The United States Supreme Court used a solid 5-to-4 conservative majority to prevent the full implementation of the civil rights laws.

It was against this background that George W. Bush became President of the United States as the result of the brazen theft of the 2000 presidential election. The United States Supreme Court actively colluded in that theft by means of a historic 5-to-4 decision in which Justice Sandra Day O'Connor cast the deciding vote in a partisan decision that was based on questionable law, contradicting her previous consistent votes in favor of states' rights.

She also maintained her solidarity with Anthony Kennedy, the other conservative justice, and William Renquist, Antonin Scalia, and Clarence Thomas, the three ultraconservative justices, with whom she has voted on virtually every significant political or economic case that came before the Court during her tenure. Only on social issues, such as partial-birth abortion, affirmative action in university admissions, and separation of church and state has she occasionally voted with the three liberal justices (John Paul Stevens, Stephen Breyer, and Ruth Ginsberg) and the one centrist (David Souter).

On cases of critical interest to Blacks, such as the death penalty, affirmative action in federal contracts for minority contractors, gun control in school zones, redistricting for the purpose of electing Black candidates, vouchers for religious-school tuition, and the Florida recount in the 2000 election, she voted with the ultraconservatives.

In one of the most recent cases to come before the Court—a case of eminent domain involving the compensated appropriation of private property on behalf of the public interest—Justice O'Connor joined the three ultraconservatives in a minority opinion upholding the primacy of private property rights over the public interest.

From the Black viewpoint, Justice O'Connor is an unwavering conservative who consistently ruled against our interests, rather than a swing voter. Moreover, she played an essential role in establishing the legal foundation for the political excesses of the Bush Administration.

The presidency of George W. Bush has put in place an administration whose principal economic policies have all worked against the interests of the majority of Blacks.

The emphasis on "free trade" and globalization has led to a massive outsourcing of jobs plus a large-scale departure of United States manufacturing plants to foreign countries. The attendant loss of millions of United States jobs has hit Black workers the hardest, doubling the Black unemployment rate compared to the rate for whites.

The Bush Administration and the Republican-dominated Congress are not interested in ending racial discrimination in employment. On the contrary, they are intent on preventing the effective enforcement of the civil rights laws and ultimately repealing them. They are also doing everything they can to weaken unions, especially those that have campaigned most effectively against discrimination in the workplace.

The key to countering these policies lies in the expansion of job opportunities throughout the economy by compelling the repeal of all free-trade agreements and the penalization of all outsourcing of United States jobs.

The policy of aggressive "deregulation" of all businesses, large and small, has given license to corporations to exploit both their workforce and consumers unfairly without fear of effective government or legal intervention. Theft on the enormous scale of the Enron scandal has been made relatively easy.

The best way to combat this error is by compelling strict federal regulation of all businesses through political pressure, support for union organizing drives, and the organization of consumer boycotts.

The Bush Administration is rapidly downsizing the federal work force while simultaneously undermining the union rights of federal employees in the name of homeland security.

Since the public sector employs a disproportionately high number of Black workers and needs to expand in order to rebuild our nation's crumbling physical infrastructure, this policy can be opposed successfully by compelling a radical expansion of the public sector and supporting the union organizing drives of the Association of Federal, State, County and Municipal Employees (AFSCME).

An additional, more sweeping proposal would be to demand the institution of a universal draft by lottery of the entire population between the ages of eighteen and forty-five. Service would be for two years, with a choice of: (1) serving on United States territory only; (2) serving anywhere in the world, but only in noncombat zones; (3) *volunteering* for service in combat zones; (4) *volunteering* for five-year service as a United Nations peacekeeper; (5) serving in the reserve national guard for ten years.

The benefits would be four years of free college or graduate-school education, including books and living expenses, and lifetime full coverage of all medical, dental, and prescription drug bills. Moreover, anyone serving in a combat zone would not be obligated to perform reserve national guard service, and no tour of duty could be extended beyond the two-year service limit. The rules would apply under all circumstances except in time of a general war declared by Congress.

Such a program would result in enormous net savings because a reconstituted armed forces Corps of Engineers and Quartermaster Corps would perform at minimum cost all of the tasks now being outsourced to private contractors at fantastically high prices.[2]

In World War II, many Blacks in the segregated United States armed forces, though largely relegated to the Corps of Engineers, the Quartermaster Corps, and the Seabees, made the best use of their opportunities by mastering the skills involved in their seemingly mundane tasks. After the war, they applied these skills in relatively high-paying industrial jobs. Today, with the manufacturing industry shrinking rapidly and industrial jobs disappearing at a frighteningly high rate, the revival of the armed forces' construction and reconstruction roles would result in a vital expansion of opportunities for the entire United States working class.

In January, 2001, the Bush administration announced the projection of the Congressional Budget Office's ten-year surplus of 5.6 trillion dollars. In January 2005 the ten-year economic forecast was based on a record-high deficit of 4 trillion dollars. That's a deficit increase of 9.6 trillion dollars!! This enormous fiscal burden institutionalizes major long-term cuts in the socially targeted public spending upon which many low-wage employees are forced to rely.

The Bush tax cuts were the main factor causing the onset of this fiscal catastrophe. They converted an increasing job rate of 236,000 per month into a decline of 69,000 per month. The only significant direct benefits accrued to those with incomes over 1 million dollars—they received a 4.4 percent annual increase in their income.

Everyone else suffered from the lack of funds available for public spending, caused by the significant reduction in tax revenue. President Bush's 2006 budget cuts everything from health care to job training drastically, and such programs are the ones most vital to the great majority of Blacks. Black civil rights leaders continue to ignore this concentrated assault on Black economic interests.

White political leadership as a whole has likewise failed to oppose the Bush administration's radical implementation of President Ronald Reagan's "supply-side" economics. White liberals-turned-neoliberals opportunistically proclaim themselves to be "socially liberal but fiscally conservative." This is a cynical euphemism designed to cover up a complete sellout of both their working-class and middle-class constituencies.

The realistic threshold for a fully middle-class lifestyle for a household has risen to at least $75,000 in annual income. Therefore, the real middle class amounts to only 18 percent of the United States population, with an additional 2 percent comprising the upper class. This 20 percent of

American households having annual incomes above $75,000 accounts for 80 percent of income after taxes. The wealthy 2 percent of the total population accounts for about one-half of this amount, or 40 percent of the total national income.

Since those living below the poverty level constitute 18 percent of the total population, the working class constitutes 62 percent of the total population (80 percent minus 18 percent). This working-class majority is compelled to share 20 percent of the total national income with the poor who are the neediest of all.

Black Americans are collectively worse off than this national average implies. The Black poverty rate is almost double the white rate; Blacks are virtually absent from the ranks of the 2 percent wealthy class, and there is a 7-to-1 wealth gap between the average white and Black households. In addition, the wealth gap between the Black middle class and the Black working class is at a record high and growing.

The wealthy class, aided by an incessant barrage of brainwashing media propaganda and the sacred myth of America's unlimited opportunity for everyone to make the rags-to-riches journey, has managed to sell the middle class a manifestly unfair income distribution by purchasing the loyalty of both the white and Black entrepreneurial middle classes.

In these circumstances, Bush's economic policies have so far encountered little resistance. The professional middle class is shrinking rapidly as private-sector white-collar jobs are outsourced and public-sector jobs are eliminated. The working class has been too politically weakened and economically battered to resist effectively, and many of the poor have lost hope. Mass movements for social or political change have been out of style for over two decades. Any revival of mass political activism requires ideological and political renewal.

In contrast to the steady decline in the economic status of the Black working class, the economic status of the Black entrepreneurial class has risen at a rapid rate during the Bush years. Between 1997 and 2002, the total number of Black small businesses increased by 45 percent from 830,000 to 1,200,000. Little wonder that this segment of the Black community is not inclined toward mass political protest.

However, Black small-business ownership of 1.2 million companies lags far behind white ownership of 23 million companies—a 19-fold gap compared to an 8-fold population gap (the Black population is about 35 million out of a total population of 290 million). Hispanics, with a population about equal in size to the Black population, own 33 percent more small businesses (1.6 million). Thus, entrepreneurial Blacks have a long way to go to catch up. It would seem that, even from a purely self-interested standpoint, they have sold themselves far too cheaply.

It has been largely forgotten that the civil rights movement of the 1960s incorporated a powerful thrust for economic justice. Rev. Martin Luther King, Jr.'s "I Have a Dream" speech at the 1963 March on Washington contained far more content than the idea reflected in the incessantly repeated excerpt that I call the dream sequence. It included the following memorable lines:

> Not long after talking about that dream, I started seeing it turn into a nightmare, as I moved through the ghettos of the nation and saw my Black brothers and sisters perishing on a lonely island of poverty in

the midst of a vast ocean of material prosperity. This is no time to take the tranquilizing drug of gradualism. *Now* is the time to make real the promises of democracy. *Now* is the time to open the doors of opportunity to all of God's children.

This focus was reflected in the subsequent shift of the King movement's priorities toward economic issues, as well as in King's Poor People's March and his trip to Memphis to support that city's sanitation workers. Now, almost forty years later, economic priorities have returned to the forefront. It is time for the universal demands of economic justice, human rights, and full human dignity to occupy a position of priority above the narrow demands of racial justice, set-asides for Black businesses, and reparations for slavery.

We are at a historic crossroads where we must make clear choices, unite a majority, and move forward together, claiming what is justly ours, getting what we can take, and keeping what we can hold. Above all, we must never lose our faith in a better tomorrow.

NOTES

1. This piece of judicial and legislative sophistry has sparked an understandable but diversionary Black response. The demand of a small but vocal minority of African-Americans for reparations as back pay for past slave labor, although symbolically positive, is highly impractical.

   According to "Harper's Index" in *Harper's* magazine, the estimated number of hours of labor performed by Black slaves between 1619 and 1865 is 222,505,000. The estimated value of that labor, compounded at 6 percent interest through 1993, is 97-trillion-one-hundred-billion dollars. This amounts to 2-million-seven-hundred-and-seventy-thousand dollars owed to every African-American alive today who is descended from a United States slave. Full compensation would mean that we owned the nation. However, we would then be obligated to hand it over to the surviving Native Americans, since genocide clearly takes priority over slave labor.

Moreover, all African-Americans who are not descended from United States slaves, including those descended from freedmen, would be excluded.

A far more effective and practical demand would be constitutional recognition that slavery was a crime against humanity, plus the modification of the Fourteenth Amendment to the United States Constitution to mandate federal enforcement of the equal-protection clause.

2. During World War II, the United States Army Engineers and Seabees and their Russian counterparts virtually rebuilt the infrastructures of entire small nations as their armies were advancing. A small fraction of over $100 billion that has been wasted on the "reconstruction" of Iraq without significant results could have been used by a couple of divisions of modern Army Engineers and Seabees to rebuild Iraq's entire infrastructure over the past two years. These units were also combat-skilled experts at securing what they had built against enemy infiltration or direct attack.

CHAPTER V

CLASS COMMANDS

Class, in the form of economic and social status, has over-taken the issue of *race* per se. Although this reality has been asserting itself ever since the civil rights laws of the 1960s were enacted, most Black leaders have clung to the out-moded premise that race *alone* is the primary issue affecting the vital interests of their constituency as a whole. Economic issues are given secondary status, whereas they are insepara-bly intertwined with the issue of race.

The refined, post-civil rights forms of racial discrimination are embedded in the economic policies, ideology, and infras-tructure of United States society. I believe that W. E. B. DuBois's well-confirmed assertion that America's problem of the twentieth century was "the color line" should be updated to acknowledge that America's twin problems of the twenty-first century are the color line *and* the class line.

The failure of middle-class Black leadership to identify and respond to this interconnection between race and class reflects a conscious collusion between a majority of the Black middle class and the white establishment to cover up the centrality of class within both the Black and white con-stituencies. The "free-market," "free-trade," "supply-side" economic policies that are rooted in the ideology of "priva-tization," "deregulation," and "globalization" inherently intensify racial discrimination and block its remedy by removing the governance of the economy from direct political control by the people. This leads to rule by corporations instead of government "of the people, by the people, for the people."

As a result, the wealthiest 0.01 percent of the total United States population has launched an unrestrained class war against working people that is crushing their American dream. Their upward economic mobility blocked and their expectations shattered, many are beginning to lose hope. For them, and for almost all other Americans, the quality of life is being trashed, the environment is being poisoned, and the general health is deteriorating. Their educational opportunities are thwarted by an inadequate public school system. The rising economic tide unleashed by a tiny class of plutocrats threatens to sink a great many ships. And since the Black ships are the most vulnerable, they are the first to go under.

To compel this tide to recede, it is necessary to use political power, combined with mass action, including nonviolent civil disobedience, as twin weapons in the struggle for equal economic opportunity *plus* an equitable share of economic benefits. However, the Black leadership has restricted the use of political power to negotiations at their level for minor economic concessions benefiting the Black middle and upper classes.

Political challenges to the unfair economic status quo have been avoided, and mass political action has been discouraged with the sole exception of voter registration. The overall strategy of Black leadership can be described as an update of Booker T. Washington's accomodationism laced with touches of symbolic cultural nationalism.

The result has been an increasing bankruptcy of Black leadership, accompanied by a dramatic rise in the relative economic status of the top 25 percent of Black Americans and a steady decline in the economic status of the other 75 percent. If the status quo, or anything close to it, is maintained, we as a people will never catch up economically.

There is good reason for the flawed choice of priorities by a large part of Black leadership: the Bush administration pays handsomely for accomodationism. Enormous payoffs have been made available to the Black elite, partly under the hypocritical banner of the "faith-based initiative," in return for an abdication of leadership in the struggle to improve the status of the Black majority.

Matters have reached the point where one of the wealthiest Black celebrities can find supportive Black audiences for his attacks on poor Black parents for spending too much on expensive sneakers and not enough on books for their children. This criticism has merit, but the view that Dr. Bill Cosby's blanket critiques of poor Blacks constitute "tough love" or "truth telling" is unconvincing in light of Cosby's failure to address the immense social and economic problems that burden the people he tends to ridicule. The time has come to oppose those members of the Black elite who pursue the interests of the middle-class minority of Blacks at the expense of the majority.

The thinking of the civil rights leadership has remained confined to the concepts of the civil rights struggle of the 1960s. Unlike Rev. Martin Luther King, Jr., who in 1967 and 1968 shifted his focus from civil rights to equal opportunity and from racial issues to economic issues, most of the current Black leadership has been unable or unwilling to challenge the inherent inadequacies of the 1965 Civil Rights Act by initiating a mass struggle for equal opportunity.

Such a struggle is necessitated by the continued denial of equal opportunity for Blacks. This denial is made possible by the absence of any legal mechanism for outlawing today's rampant *unofficial* racial discrimination. Institutions, corporations, and small businesses discriminate extensively without fear of prosecution because the 1965 Civil Rights Act outlawed *legal* (official) segregation but not *de facto* (unofficial) segregation.

In the year prior to his assassination in 1968, Rev. King asserted that the Black revolution was more than "a struggle for the rights of Negroes." It had become a struggle to deal with "the problem of the gulf between the haves and the have-nots." By contrast, today's civil rights leadership has enshrined Rev. King's outdated 1963 "I Have a Dream" speech and ignored his currently pertinent admonitions of 1967 and 1968.

What is urgently required is the clear definition of Black class interests and the development of a program to pursue those interests. This requires a struggle for *equal opportunity* rather than empty rhetoric about civil rights that have long since been won. A direct challenge to present institutional discrimination is called for in a situation where a strong racist undercurrent persists among white Americans, and popular support for the redress of either past or present racial discrimination has all but vanished.

■ ■ ■

The goal of equal opportunity can best be achieved by preserving and redirecting affirmative-action programs and can be mounted only within a broader context of expanding job opportunities, growth of labor unions, and regulation of corporations. In such an environment, affirmative action can provide an avenue for shifting the political ground to a broad assault on *present* discrimination against all minorities; for changing the focus of the political debate from aid to "disadvantaged" individual victims of past discrimination to equal opportunity for all members of minority groups, and for establishing economic fairness, rather than race, as the number-one issue in the 2006 and 2008 elections.

Such a campaign should have several aspects:

1. A reassessment of the group interests of African-Americans should unequivocally give priority to the interests of the Black working class, instead of the interests of the Black middle class, and should emphasize group interest rather than individual interest.

2. The civil rights movement should be replaced by an equal-opportunity movement whose goal is equal opportunity for all Americans regardless of race, and whose strategy includes the use of mass nonviolent action.

3. The legal framework within which affirmative-action issues are contested should be revised.

The legal purpose of affirmative action programs should be redefined as a remedy exclusively for *present* discrimination by the majority group against members of *minority groups*. It should be excluded as a remedy for any other purpose, such as compensation for past discrimination, the redress of social and economic disadvantage, or the establishment of diversity. These excluded purposes are vitally important ones, but they should be addressed more directly by programs other than affirmative action. Moreover, the paramount issue of present social and economic disadvantage has remained virtually untouched by current affirmative action programs.

Therefore, quotas, which have been declared illegal by decision of the United States Supreme Court, should be understood to refer only to the remedy for *past* discrimination. This new definition of a quota would legalize mandatory numerical results in the hiring or acceptance of all minorities, regardless of their qualifications, to remedy *present* discrimination.

The "strict scrutiny" standard should be applied to the search for present, rather than past, discrimination. In addition, the *equal treatment clause of the Fourteenth Amendment* should be explicitly established as the single standard of review and judgment of affirmative-action cases by the federal government as the final arbiter.

4. Those who wish to abolish affirmative action programs should be cast publicly as defenders of ongoing discrimination against all minorities, whereas the supporters of affirmative action should be deemed opponents of discrimination against all minorities rather than as defenders of "racial preferences."

What has become primarily a Black issue must be transformed into a minority issue. Success in advancing Black interests in the struggle to preserve affirmative action requires a coalition with other minorities and with economically disadvantaged whites. This means that affirmative action must incorporate a decisive economic factor by favoring low-income minorities.

5. The group interests of Black Americans require that the focus in United States politics be shifted significantly from the race issue to the issue of economic fairness.

To accomplish this shift, Black leadership should emphasize the economic interests of the Black working class and the strategy of coalitions based on economic issues, rather than purely racial demands. Such a policy entails considerable moral and political courage, since it requires frontal opposition to the significant nationalist trend in the community.

For example, a Black mass march on Washington, D.C. on the tenth anniversary of the Million Man March should embrace the theme of Black political empowerment for the purpose of achieving equal opportunity. The twin theme of economic fairness, modeled after President Franklin D. Roosevelt's New Deal, should be the basis for reaching out to all working people.

6. Women are a majority of the population, even though they are heavily discriminated against. Therefore, they should not be classified as a "minority." Discrimination against women as a group should be dealt with separately from discrimination against "racial minorities" or "ethnic minorities." The remedies for all types of discrimination should be *mandatory federally enforced minimum quotas* based on the goal of equitable representation within a short time frame.

This issue is of prime importance to Blacks, Latinos, Asians, and white women alike. Affirmative action as currently applied has produced a sharp division between white women and ethnic minorities. White women have benefited the most but have been kept well below equality with white men. The Black working class and the poor, whose need is the greatest, have benefited the least.

■　■　■

The positive effects of affirmative action for Blacks have been minimized by both lack of education and lack of opportunity. Compared to whites, Blacks suffer from double the poverty rate, double the unemployment rate, and almost double the high-school dropout rate. Barely half of Black high-school students graduate with a regular diploma, and only one in five is prepared for college.

These conditions are a direct result of the Republican economic policies that have been almost completely dominant under Republican presidents during sixteen of the past twenty-five years. Only the eight years of the two Clinton administrations averted a far greater disaster.

The concealed purpose of current Republican economic policies is to create a large and permanent underclass that can be exploited at will. In such circumstances, unions will all but vanish, or at least be so weakened as to be ineffectual. In response to this clear and present threat, a complacent, business-as-usual Black leadership continues to parrot the traditional mainstream myth of the United States as the great land of opportunity. As if brainwashed by the media-corporate elite, they offer the spent strategy of individual self-reliance, education, cultural assimilation, and entrepreneurship as the *only* available tools for advancement of "the race."

Bruce S. Gordon, the new President of the NAACP, is a prime example of this leadership stance. A retired executive of the Verizon Company, Mr. Gordon was chosen by the NAACP board of directors because of his thirty-five years of corporate marketing experience. His primary assignment is to "push the NAACP toward a more economic-based approach to civil rights, including . . . prodding pension funds and corporations to hire more black [sic] managers." Gordon was also quoted as saying that he would raise money for an endowment, setting a goal of $200 million dollars.[1]

An "economic-based approach to civil rights" is a contradictory concept. Civil rights are *politically based* Constitutional citizenship rights that are designed to enable every individual citizen to achieve a better life on a reasonably level playing field. These rights were achieved and can be preserved by *political means only*. There is no direct *legal* connection between economics and politics except for the ability of constitutionally exercised political power to control economics. Civil rights include political rights but not economic rights.

Of course, money consistently buys politicians *illegally*, and therefore the wealthy can always buy an unfairly large voice in government policy. But this very condition points to the futility of any attempt by Black Americans, who constitute an economically weak and disadvantaged minority, to achieve political results by economic means.

The hiring of more Black managers and the goal of a $200 million NAACP endowment is unrelated to the interests of the Black working class and poor. Such priorities are exclusively those of the Black entrepreneurial middle class, whom the results would benefit. Priorities such as jobs, health care, minimum wage, better public education, and more Black professionals are omitted.

Funding the education of low-income Blacks would appear to be a far nobler endeavor than accumulating an endowment. And since there is an acute shortage of Black teachers at a time of crisis in Black education, an ideal undertaking for the NAACP might be a large-scale investment in the recruiting and training of Black teachers for the public school system.

A July 30, 2005, article in the *New York Times* education supplement reported that fewer highly qualified people are entering the teaching profession, and the number of minority teachers remains disproportionately low. About 40 percent of the nationwide public school population is minority, whereas 84 percent of the teachers are white, 8 percent are Black, 6 percent are Latino, and 1.6 percent are Asian; 14 percent of teachers leave the profession in their first year and 46 percent by the fifth year.

Over the next five years, 500,000 new teachers will be needed to offset the growing student population and the accelerated retirement rate of the teachers. A highly productive undertaking for the NAACP would be spearheading the recruitment and training of at least 100,000 Black teachers by the end of 2010.

Mr. Gordon does express the irrefutably correct view that "We've got to get the right emphasis placed on economic equality. I happen to think that when you have economic stability and equality, that often becomes an enabler for social equality." However, while Gordon emphasizes the goal of social equality, he ignores the debilitating social conditions that must be remedied in order to achieve it.

In response to questions raised by "civil rights advocates," who emphasized the need for the NAACP to clarify its *mission*, Gordon responded that "When you advertise, you communicate your company's products and services. You don't advertise, people don't get the message. . . . We need to promote the NAACP for what it is, what it stands for."

Revealingly, Gordon makes no reference to a *mission*, because the NAACP ceased to have a mission at the moment the Civil Rights Act of 1965 was enacted, effectively terminating the civil rights *movement*. A movement is a mass phenomenon requiring a clear and inspiring mission. Without the mission, there can be no movement in any real sense. And without a movement based on the strength of an ethnic group, there can be no organized national leadership of the group as a whole. Only competing factions can function in such circumstances.

The civil rights movement demonstrated that political power exercised by means of a movement pursuing a mission having a broad popular appeal can yield substantial results. On this point, Mr. Gordon's supporters claim that "his lack of overt political activity and his strong corporate experience will make it easier for him to work with Republicans, particularly President Bush." Gordon said that "reaching out" to the White House was one of his top immediate priorities. "I think there have to be common issues between the NAACP and the current administration." Since the Black working class and poor share no common interests with the current administration, it is reasonable to conclude that Gordon is speaking exclusively for the Black middle class.

Thus, the NAACP presents itself as "the leading civil rights organization" while actually serving as a political lobbying group for the Black entrepreneurial middle class.

Julian Bond, the chairman of the NAACP board, stated that Gordon's life experience made him ideally suited to help guide the evolving civil rights movement. "As opportunity has increased, it has become possible for there to be a range of ways ... you could have an impact on civil rights," Bond added.

Mr. Bond's comments are based on illusions rather than on reality. Contrary to his assertion that "opportunity has increased," it has decreased dramatically for at least 75 percent of the American people. It has increased mainly for entrepreneurs and professionals. For the Black working class and poor, it has all but vanished.

There can be no evolving *Black* civil rights movement, since its mission of civil rights for Black Americans was completed by the enactment of the 1965 Civil Rights Act. Today's rights mission has become that of *human* rights, which explicitly include *economic* rights.

In popular terms, this mission can be defined as the establishment of Franklin D. Roosevelt's first two freedoms—freedom from want and freedom from fear—as Constitutional birthrights of every citizen. Thus, the human-rights movement is simultaneously a movement for economic rights and for peace. These missions conform to those embraced by Rev. Martin Luther King *after* the enactment of the 1965 Civil Rights Act—his Poor People's March and his opposition to the Vietnam War.

■　■　■

The Black working class has chosen to pursue its advancement primarily by joining the manufacturing, service, and transportation unions—the progressive wing of the labor movement formerly constituting the Congress of Industrial Organization (CIO). The relatively conservative former American Federation of Labor (AFL) unions have a history of segregation and generally do not share the priorities of the Black working class. Consequently, Black workers, and especially Black women, wield a powerful influence within the former CIO unions.

At present, a major crisis has erupted within the leadership of the AFL-CIO over the direction the labor movement should take. The cause of the upheaval is the failure of the present leadership under AFL-CIO President John Sweeney to halt the perilous decline of the labor movement. Today, only 13 percent of nonagricultural workers are unionized. Only 18 percent of the total workforce is unionized—just half the 1955 peak of 35 percent after the AFL-CIO merger. Most of the pensions and fringe benefit programs that were in place only a few years ago have now been abandoned by employers. Wage cuts and speed-ups are continually being imposed against only token resistance. Free trade and globalization have deprived millions of their jobs and threaten millions more.

In response to this crisis, several key unions from the former CIO are demanding major policy and organizational changes in the AFL-CIO. These changes include a new president with a fresh view, a doubling of the current budget for organizing nonunion workers, and consolidation of all member unions on the principle of a single union per industry. The leaders of the dissenting unions, who represent over a third of the AFL-CIO's 13 million members, have threatened to secede from the AFL-CIO as a bloc if their radical reforms are not adopted at the annual convention in Chicago. They call themselves the Change to Win Coalition and have decided not to attend the convention.

Their sweeping reform proposals would merge industry unions in order to make it harder for employers to pit unions against each other. They would pursue the goals of doubling the number of unionized workers, raising both hourly wages and the minimum wage, and restoring pension and health benefits. They would also launch a sustained political campaign to achieve an updated version of Franklin D. Roosevelt's union-friendly New Deal political and economic order.

Black Americans have an enormous stake in the outcome of this crisis, since Black workers have suffered the most from the decline of the labor movement. All of the reforms advocated by the dissenting unions are entirely in the collective interests of Black workers. Yet the present leadership of the Black trade-union movement is mired in a misguided, narrowly conceived centrist position at this historic juncture.

At the recent convention of the Coalition of Black Trade Unionists, its president, William Lucy, told several thousand Black trade unionists that he is anxious for Black workers not to be taken for granted by the labor movement. "Whether we are accepted by the powerful players in labor or the Democratic Party or not, we will continue to come to the aid of unorganized workers, and we will continue to mobilize our communities." These remarks are both misplaced and irrelevant to the main issue currently facing Black trade unionists in the labor movement.

Since the June 27, 2005 meeting of the AFL-CIO executive council overwhelmingly endorsed a resolution to expand leadership diversity, "the powerful players in labor" clearly do not take Black workers for granted. Black representation at all leadership levels of the labor movement, though insufficient, is already far greater than in any other mainstream institution in the United States.

On the political front, Lucy endorsed the political tone set by Rev. Jesse Jackson who asserted that "We must build an independent political struggle that will define the priorities and behavior of both political parties." This is the traditional position of the Black middle class and conflicts with the interests of the overwhelming majority of the Black population.[2]

Since 90 percent or more of all Black voters, and an even higher percentage of Black trade unionists, consistently vote for the Democratic Party, Blacks have no interest in defining the priorities and behavior of the Republican Party. They have no ability to do so in any case, since the Republican Party represents their corporate adversaries and openly appeals to white racists. On the other hand, Black trade unionists already wield a decisive influence in defining the priorities and behavior of the Democratic Party.

The Republican Party, with its Southern strategy appealing to its racist base of southern whites and its consistently antilabor legislative and enforcement policies, is the main political enemy of African-Americans as an ethnic group. It is not in our interests to negotiate with our political enemies except from a position of partisan political power. Consequently, all civil rights leaders, politicians, and union leaders, without exception, who negotiate with the Bush administration from a position of political neutrality for any reason, are never doing so in our interest.

The leadership of the two leading civil rights organizations—the NAACP and the National Urban League (NUL)—have permanently embraced a position of political neutrality in order to guarantee their tax-exempt status. As a result, they are politically irrelevant to the advancement of Black political interests. They cannot oppose our main political enemy, the Republican Party, nor can they support our main political ally, the Democratic Party.

Therefore, they cannot advance the political interests of the Black working class in any direct way. Focusing exclusively on advancing the narrow political interests of the Black middle class, they court President George Bush and accept major charitable donations from the corporations that finance the Republican Party.

Thus, Black trade unionists should focus primarily on advancing the interests of the Black working class by functioning as an independent Black caucus within the labor movement on the basis of policies decided by their own majority. In the present context, it is clear that their overall interests are best served by supporting the position of the dissenting unions, especially since these unions have a heavily Black membership and a track record on racial issues that shames the far more conservative former AFL unions. The labor movement is sorely in need of a fresh new leadership with a bold vision for the future.

NOTES

1. News story in the *New York Times*, July 5, 2005.
2. The *New York Amsterdam News*, July 21–July 27, 2005.

CHAPTER VI

VOTE FRAUD IN 2000 AND 2004

The pervasive inconsistencies in the official 2000 and 2004 election results raise serious questions concerning the integrity of the American electoral system and the honesty of federal and state government. These inconsistencies are doubly disturbing because they constitute a distinct and repetitive pattern that implies a preplanned manipulation of millions of votes after they had been initially processed.

The deliberate and insistent manner in which the mainstream media have ignored glaring evidence of major differences between the exit polls and the official results in both the 2000 and 2004 elections is dismaying confirmation of pervasive media corruption. In these circumstances, a continued investigation and public debate of proven election irregularities, biased election procedures, and documented voter suppression is mandatory. Meaningful democracy cannot exist without a fair and reliable electoral system. In my view, our present system has failed dismally in two successive pivotal presidential elections. As a result, both the system and the President have lost the trust of a substantial portion of the American people at a critical historical juncture.

THE 2000 ELECTION: FLAWED SYSTEM
OR HIGHWAY ROBBERY?

In 2000, the electoral college system awarded the election to George W. Bush despite Al Gore's official popular vote lead of 500,000 votes. The loser graciously conceded, pledging fealty to the winner; the anxious public heaved a sigh of relief, and the mass media effectively suppressed all attempts to revisit the issue of possible election fraud.

Following that election, large expenditures and extensive efforts were made to improve the electoral system. However, despite near-universal acknowledgement of widespread abuses and systemic flaws that were prevalent throughout the 2000 election process, none of the filed charges of felony vote fraud were sustained. Inexcusably, no significant improvements were made in a deeply flawed electoral system.

My investigation of the official returns for the 2000 and 2004 presidential elections reveals a clear pattern of vote manipulation in 2000 that was repeated and expanded in 2004. Consequently, a detailed examination of the 2000 voting patterns is essential to an understanding of the 2004 results.

The composite exit-poll estimate of the 2000 presidential voting returns differed widely from the official results for the first time in the history of exit polls. The predicted decisive Gore victory by 2.8 million popular votes was reduced to a thin 0.5-million-vote margin in the official count. A focus on ethnic groups (white, Black, Hispanic, and Asian) reveals the manner in which this questionable change occurred.

An investigation is continuing with regard to alleged illegal invalidation and/or suppression (by official and unofficial intimidation) of at least 1.0 million Black votes in 2000. In addition to the manipulation of the Black vote, many ballots were invalidated because of errors made by the electronic machines. Others were counted in the initial count, only to be invalidated in the mandatory second count or revalidated in the recount.

Therefore the total number of valid ballots is still in dispute, since it depends on the disputed number of invalidated ballots deducted from the fixed 111.0 million certified total number of ballots cast.

The pattern and result of the changes made by the official count suggest a preplanned nationwide vote manipulation executed from a central headquarters with disciplined precision under cover of a massive disinformation campaign and followed by a massive cover-up operation. The very idea that such a vast conspiracy, exceeding by far the vote fraud that occurred in the recent Ukrainian presidential elections, could occur in the United States seems preposterous to most Americans. It is usually dismissed as the babble of those obsessed with "conspiracy theories" and/or the sinister workings of "enemy propaganda." However, this very fact appears to have made it terrifyingly simple to perpetrate.

The composite exit polls correctly predicted a Gore victory over Bush by 52.7 million to 49.9 million (49.4 percent to 46.8 percent)—a margin of 2.8 million popular votes. The fraudulent official result was a Gore majority in the popular vote by 0.5 million votes (48.4 percent to 47.9 percent), coupled with a Bush victory in the electoral college.

This official fraud was perpetrated on electronic voting machines that provided no verifying receipt and were controlled by Republican electoral commissions. According to widely published official reports, about 40.0 million votes out of the 111.0 million total were cast on these electronic machines, which were highly vulnerable to cheating.

The fraudulent switching of Black votes was especially egregious. About 0.2 million Black votes that had been cast for Nader were officially not counted (i.e., "lost") after being switched to Bush, increasing his total from 49.9 million to 50.1 million, and his share of the Black vote from 6 percent to 8 percent. In addition, the Black vote for Gore was reduced from the 92 percent predicted by the exit polls to 90 percent. This "loss" reduced his total by about 0.2 million votes from 52.7 million to 52.5 million.

At least 1.1 million counted Black votes were illegally invalidated and then switched to the white category. (They could not be switched directly, since the Black and white votes were cast in different locations, often on different kinds of machines.) Consequently, the total Black vote was reduced by 1 percent from 11 percent to 10 percent of the overall total, while the white vote was increased from 77 percent to 78 percent. Since the white vote favored Bush by 54 percent to 42 percent, this switch of Black votes to white votes increased Bush's total from 50.1 million to 50.5 million, and decreased Gore's total from 52.5 million to 52.0 million.

Finally, 1.0 million white Gore votes were invalidated, reducing his total from 52.0 million to 51.0 million.

These manipulations with 0.2 (Black votes "lost" and then switched) + 1.1 (Black votes illegally invalidated and then switched) + 1.0 (white votes invalidated) for a total of 2.3 million votes were covered up by a series of alterations within the invalid-vote category.[1]

The total number of 4.3 million actual invalid votes was increased by 1.3 million to the improbably high figure of 5.6 million.

Having thus reduced Gore's actual popular vote lead of 2.8 million votes to 0.5 million, the Bush campaign stole the electoral college vote in Florida, and the United States

Supreme Court gave its blessing to the second-largest vote heist in modern history. (The largest one was to come in 2004.)

■ ■ ■

The stories about voting fraud that surfaced nationwide immediately after the 2000 election were dismissed by the mainstream media as sour grapes and conspiracy theories. After all, how could any patriotic American even imagine that our "free and open" society could possibly tolerate such highway robbery in broad daylight? Political thuggery of this kind could happen only in "authoritarian countries" or "banana republics." "Besides," the media chorused, "the exit polls were inaccurate" and had to be corrected when later returns came in.

But wait a minute. No evidence has turned up to show that the early exit polls were inaccurate. The theft of Black votes occurred in states where Republicans were in total control of the entire electoral machinery and also controlled the state courts. Most of the electronic voting machines were manufactured and serviced by a company owned by Republicans. The television stations that led the reversal of the exit polls were controlled by Republicans.

Moreover, a majority of white Americans do not even want to contemplate what a majority of Blacks believe but do not say—that the Bush administration harbors a gang of neoconservative racist political thugs who will employ any means necessary to acquire and consolidate power.

The November 9 summary in the *New York Times* published the exit-poll vote percentages by ethnic group, along with the official 48 percent–48 percent dead-heat result. However, if the result is calculated on the basis of the ethnic-group percentages in the same summary, the result is a 49.4 percent–46.8 percent (52.7 million–49.9 million) Gore win by 2.8 million popular votes (the number of actual valid votes was 106.7 million).

The November 12 summary published the same 48 percent–48 percent dead-heat official result and the officially "adjusted" ethnic-group vote percentages. Here the calculations based on the ethnic-group vote closely match the result: Gore 48.4 percent vs. Bush 47.9 percent (51.0 million–50.5 million)—a Gore win by a mere 0.5 million popular votes. (The number of official valid votes was only 105.4 million, 1.3 million less than the actual number. This reflects the 1.3 million extra invalid votes.)

The *Times* published both summaries without editorial comment. Was the *Times* part of a cover-up operation?

THE 2004 ELECTION: WAS IT INSULT ADDED TO INJURY?

In the 2004 election, the manipulation of recorded votes by the same predominantly white, conservative, Republican election officials replicated the pattern used to determine the outcome of the 2000 election. Massive numbers of minority votes were shifted or invalidated in a manner designed to increase Bush's vote and decrease Kerry's. About 900,000 Black and Hispanic votes were switched from Kerry to Bush, and approximately 2.1 million Hispanic votes were invalidated and reclassified as white votes.

Despite all of these manipulations, the outcome of the 2004 election hinged on the popular vote in the State of Ohio. Here Kerry's predicted substantial lead of about

250,000 votes vanished, and Bush "won" by about *120,000* votes. This result was apparently achieved by switching *370,000* Kerry votes to the Bush column.

Partial evidence of this fraud was revealed by Ohio Secretary of State J. Kenneth Blackwell when he stated in a *New York Times* interview that *93,000 out of 5.7 million* total valid Ohio ballots did not indicate a vote for president. This would mean that *1.7 percent* of Ohio voters chose to vote for "none of the above" in casting their presidential ballot—a virtual impossibility because the nationwide percentage of this ballot category was only *0.17 percent.*

Of the fourteen states in which Black votes were switched, nine are controlled by Republican governors. This fact made it relatively easy for Black Republicans to manipulate Black votes cast in predominantly Black neighborhoods. In addition, some prominent Black ministers in these states were bribed by the Bush campaign to sell the false Republican claim that in 2004 Black voters shifted significantly toward Bush on the basis of their opposition to gay marriage.

Reliable figures confirm that the 91 percent Black Democratic vote in 2004 was virtually the same as the 92 percent in 2000 and was based on the overwhelming Black disenchantment with Bush.

Of the nine states in which Hispanic votes were switched, the five states with the highest concentrations of Hispanic voters (California, New York, Texas, Florida, and Colorado), as well as the sixth state (Georgia), are governed by conservative Republicans. There it was easy for the Republican-dominated electoral machinery to manipulate votes with impunity. The cover-up was aided by conservative Catholic churches, who hyped the gay-marriage and abortion issues in return for extensive Republican funding, in part via Bush's "faith-based initiative."

However, both local exit polls and reliable national surveys confirm that the 2004 Hispanic vote essentially replicated the 2000 vote. Most Hispanics voted on the basis of their economic and political interests rather than in response to appeals based on moral or religious values. Bush, as an economically conservative, Anglo-Saxon, fundamentalist Protestant, failed to overcome the wide cultural gap between himself and predominantly Democratic, Catholic, economically liberal Hispanic voters.

In the other three states where significant numbers of Hispanic votes were switched, the governors are Democrats who are members of political or ethnic minorities: the governor of Arizona is a woman, the governor of New Jersey is Irish Catholic, and the governor of New Mexico is Hispanic. The probability that Hispanic voters in these states would have abandoned their commitment to the Democratic Party in significant numbers is vanishingly small.

Class-action litigation on behalf of Black and Hispanic voters in the federal courts of as many as ten states having large Black and Hispanic voting blocs can initiate a major national debate. The primary basis of the litigation should be the equal-treatment clause of the Fourteenth Amendment to the United States Constitution, and the main precedent should be the United States Supreme Court decision in the 1954 *Brown vs. Board of Education* case. The importance of this precedent resides in the fact that such cases must be heard in federal, rather than in state court, and only the federal court offers the possibility of a fair hearing in a state election fraud case.

■ ■ ■

The leaders of the current administration, including President Bush and Vice President Cheney, appear to be unscrupulous individuals who tell any lie they think they can get away with, commit any crime they are unlikely to be indicted for, and license any political thug who can aid their cause. "Opposition" leaders who fear to expose this reality of today's political landscape are leaders in name only.

The mainstream press has abdicated its journalistic responsibilities entirely by treating this betrayal of the American people as an issue to be spun, rather than as a matter involving the very survival of United States democracy. In an article published in the August 2005 issue of *Harper's* magazine by Mark Crispin Miller, titled "None Dare Call it Stolen: Ohio, the Election, and America's Servile Press," the author ends with a chilling reminder:

> In this nation's epic struggle on behalf of freedom, reason, and democracy, the press has unilaterally disarmed—and therefore many good Americans, both liberal and conservative, have lost faith in the promise of self-government. That vast surrender is demoralizing, certainly, but if we face it, and endeavor to reverse it, it will not prove fatal. This democracy can survive a plot to hijack an election. What it cannot survive is our indifference to, or unawareness of, the evidence that such a plot has succeeded.

On January 5, 2005, John Conyers, the ranking Democrat on the House Judiciary Committee, issued a Status Report of the House Judiciary Committee Democratic Staff under the title, "Preserving Democracy: What Went Wrong in Ohio." This official congressional document details and verifies a mountain of irregularities, illegal abuses of power, and out-right crimes perpetrated by the Republican Administration of the State of Ohio throughout the entire 2004 preelection, election, and postelection processes:

■ Voter turnout was suppressed by intimidation of 35,000 predominantly minority voters by means of preelection selective targeting.

■ Many thousands of voters who did not receive provisional ballots in a timely manner were prevented from receiving them at all, and were disfranchised. In addition, the issuance of provisional ballots was illegally restricted. In Cayuhoga County, 8,099 out of 24,472 provisional ballots were ruled invalid.

■ Thousands of Republican challengers, in addition to artificially created long lines and long waits, disfranchised tens of thousands of legal minority voters.

■ Tens of thousands of voters were disfranchised statewide through illegal purging of voter lists. In Cayuhoga County alone, over 10,000 Ohio citizens lost their right to vote because of registration errors committed by election officials.

■ Most of the 93,000 ballots on which no vote was cast for president had still not been reviewed by January 5, 2005. In two Montgomery County precincts that reported a suspicious undervote rate of 25 percent each, 6,000 voters who stood in line to vote would have had to decline to vote for president.

■ In Mahoning County, at least twenty-five electronic

machines transferred an unknown number of Kerry votes to the Bush column.

■ Warren County locked out public observers from vote counting, citing a nonexistent FBI terrorist warning.

■ In Cayuhoga County, little-known third party candidates received twenty times more votes than any such candidate had ever received in otherwise reliably Democratic-leaning areas.

■ In Miami County, voter turnout was a suspiciously high 98.55 percent, and after 100 percent of the precincts had been reported, 19,000 extra votes were recorded for President Bush.

■ Throughout Ohio, the voting process was chaotic, taxing, and ultimately fruitless for many in predominantly Democratic and African-American areas.

■ The voting computer company Triad has essentially admitted that it provided "cheat sheets" to those counting the ballots during the recount in numerous counties. The cheat sheets informed election officials how many votes they should find for each candidate, and how many overvotes and undervotes they should calculate to match the machine count. In that way, they could avoid doing the full countywide hand recount mandated by state law.

All sections of the mass media have been universally silent about these flagrant abuses. Instead, they have gone out of their way to ridicule and suppress all efforts to discuss them. The principal reason for this attitude resides in the wealth of evidence of media collusion in the Republican Party's theft of both the 2000 and 2004 presidential elections. They doctored their own exit polls and then refused to make public their raw data.

Prior to the election, the press generally reported Kerry's late surge accurately. It was only after the initial exit polls were reported on election day that the press caved in under Republican pressure.

For example, the *New York Times* reported in September, 2004 that new registration in Ohio rose 25 percent in predominantly Republican precincts, compared to 250 percent in predominantly Democratic precincts. Susan Page, writing in the November 1, 2004, issue of *USA Today*, reported that the swing states were leaning toward Kerry and that the polls showed Kerry and Bush tied nationally. The initial exit polls obtained by both the *New York Times* and *USA Today* showed Kerry winning by a margin ranging from 3.5 million to 5.0 million votes, yet neither newspaper questioned Bush's official "win" by 3.0 million votes.

On January 6, 2001, House Democrats led by the Congressional Black Caucus challenged the results of the 2000 presidential election as fraudulent. Their challenge failed because not a single Democratic senator chose to join them.

In January of 2005, House Democrats, again led by the Congressional Black Caucus, challenged the results of the 2004 presidential election on the grounds of systematic nationwide fraud. One member of the caucus was reprimanded by the House for accusing the Republican Party of stealing the election. This time, the challenge succeeded because Democratic Senator Barbara Boxer of California supported the challenge, forcing full debates in both houses of Congress.

Although this was a rare and powerful news story, the

Boston Globe gave it 118 words on page 3, and the *Los Angeles Times* allocated 60 words on page 18. It made no news in the *Wall Street Journal, USA Today, Newsweek, Time, U.S. News and World Report*, NPR radio, CNN, CBS, NBC, ABC, Fox News, or PBS. *The New York Times* mentioned it cursorily. Obviously, the press was part of a conspiracy of silence and coverup.

The monumental betrayal of their constituency by all of the "liberal" Democratic Party leaders is evidenced by its silence and by the congressional vote on the challenge by progressive rank-and-file House Democrats. More than 40 House Democrats voted with the Republicans against the challenge, and over 130 didn't show up. Only 31 intrepid progressive Democrats, a disproportionately high number of them from the Congressional Black Caucus, supported the challenge as it went down to defeat by a lopsided 267-to-31 margin. In the Senate, which defeated the challenge by a 74-to-1 margin, only the brave Barbara Boxer voted to support it. All 55 Republicans were joined by 19 Democrats in opposing the challenge, and 24 Democrats, including Barak Obama, the only Black senator, along with the one independent, chose not to attend.

All of this evidence, combined with my calculations in the Appendix to this book, have led me to conclude that both the 2000 and 2004 presidential elections were stolen by means of a planned, centrally directed Republican conspiracy carried out in full public view by a highly disciplined national Republican Party organization. This conspiracy was backed by the mobilized political power of the national Republican administration in direct collaboration with Republican state administrations.

I have also concluded that the Democratic Party, by refusing to fight two obvious thefts of the presidency from its presidential candidate, has demonstrated that it no longer serves as an alternative party to the Republican Party. In reality there is one center-right party in which the Republicans constitute the right wing and the Democrats constitute the left wing. There is no genuine opposition party. The "partisan" congressional conflicts are mere political games with much sound and fury, signifying very little.

Consequently, it remains for the American people to clean up the political system which has been befouled by the present corrupt political class.

NOTE

1. (A) The number of white invalid votes was increased by 2.1 million from 3.2 million to 5.3 million to account for (a) the 1.1 million Black votes that were fraudulently switched to white votes, and (b) the 1.0 million white Gore votes that were fraudulently invalidated.

(B) The number of Black invalid votes was decreased from 0.7 million to 0.1 million to cover the 0.4 million increase in Bush's white vote plus the 0.2 million Black votes for Nader that were switched to Bush and then "disappeared."

(C) About 0.2 million valid white Nader votes were invalidated and assigned to Bush, reducing Nader's total from 4.1 million to 3.9 million, and a corresponding 0.2 million white invalid Nader votes "disappeared."

(D) I have used the designation "Hispanic" rather than "Latino" in this chapter because this designation is the official one used for electoral purposes and census purposes.

CHAPTER VII

AWAITING THE FIFTH REVOLUTION

The most significant gains Blacks have achieved began with the Revolutionary War and continued through emancipation from slavery, Reconstruction during the Civil War period, the mass entry of Blacks into the Congress of Industrial Organizations (CIO) during the late 1930s and early 1940s, the desegregation of the United States Armed Forces in 1948 and the subsequent mass inclusion of Blacks in the Army and Marines, the Civil Rights Revolution culminating in the Civil Rights Act of 1965 and in the Cultural Revolution that followed it, and the rapid growth of the Black middle class during the past twenty-five years. All of these advances resulted from mass struggles led by similar political alliances.[1] Today we celebrate these results while largely forgetting or ignoring the historical contexts which made them possible.

■ ■ ■

The 1776 War of Independence and its immediate aftermath struck heavy blows against a long-entrenched nationwide slave system. Tens of thousands of southern slaves fought in or worked for the Continental Army or ran away to the North; the abolitionist movement was founded, and slavery was abolished in most northern states by 1790 (although New York and New Jersey did not do so until the early 1800s). The majority of Blacks chose to support the revolution and put their faith in its promise of freedom. Only a small minority joined the British or emigrated to Canada.

However, the promise of the Revolution was betrayed when the Constitution and Bill of Rights (the first ten amendments to the Constitution) were ratified. The vast majority of the slaves were not freed. The progressives, led by Thomas Paine, who demanded the end of slavery, universal suffrage without racial, gender, or property qualifications, the complete separation of church and state, and global peace enforced by an international confederation of republican governments, were marginalized by the liberal and conservative factions of the prerevolutionary elite.

A compromise by the liberals in the name of national unity made a mockery of the Preamble to the Constitution, which mandates government by the people "to form a more perfect union" and to "promote the general welfare." The Constitution, even with the addition of its first twelve Amendments, prevented the establishment of a "more perfect union" by legalizing slavery, embedding the principle of states' rights, and elevating property rights above human rights. It also impeded the promotion of "the general welfare" by subordinating the rights of labor to the interests of the propertied class. For example, in the Fifth Amendment to the United States Constitution, the phrase "life, liberty, or property" replaces the famous words "life, liberty, and the pursuit of happiness" which are at the core of the Declaration of Independence.

The 1790 Census revealed a total population of 3.93 million, including 880,000 slaves and 50,000 Black freedmen. These figures confirm that the great majority of Blacks remained enslaved and chose not to emigrate to Canada. Pinning their hopes for eventual freedom on the relatively weak coalition of progressives and abolitionists, they abandoned their previous trust in the liberals.

The repressive years between 1810 and 1860, marked by a continuous restriction of the rights of Blacks and a sharp increase in institutional racism, witnessed a steep rise in slave rebellions. These uprisings could not have overthrown the institution of slavery, nor was this their immediate aim. However, they were largely successful in terrorizing the white slave-owning class in much of the South. In the long run, their sacrifice arguably hastened the onset of the second American revolution—the Civil War of 1861–1865.

■ ■ ■

The election of Abraham Lincoln to the presidency in 1860 marked the beginning of the second American revolution, which demolished the Confederacy along with the institution of slavery and established the priority of freedom and people ahead of liberty and property. It overthrew, by force of a people's war, the Liberal Republic, established by the original Constitution and Bill of Rights, and replaced it with a People's Republic based on "government of the people, by the people, for the people."

President Lincoln's Emancipation Proclamation, Gettysburg Address, and Second Inaugural Address established the basis for Lincoln's Reconstruction policy, which was designed to establish this new republic. In his 1865 Inaugural Address, Lincoln underscored his demand that the Confederacy surrender unconditionally, warning that otherwise the war would continue until *"all the wealth piled by the bondsman's two hundred and fifty years of unrequited toil shall be sunk, and until every drop of blood drawn with the lash shall be paid by another drawn by the sword."*

Thus, President Abraham Lincoln was a progressive in the tradition of Thomas Paine and his path-breaking "The Rights of Man," written in 1792, rather than a liberal in the tradition of Thomas Jefferson and his 1776 "Declaration of Independence."

It was in this context that the overwhelming majority of Black Americans, both slaves and freedmen, supported Lincoln and the Union unreservedly, despite the racial discrimination they continued to face everywhere. Over 200,000 fought with the Union Army in segregated units, even though they were paid less than white soldiers. Hundreds of thousands of slaves escaped to Union lines and worked in Union labor battalions. Thousands of others aided Union intelligence, and some engaged in effective sabotage behind Confederate lines. A small but significant number of those house slaves and southern freedmen who identified with the slavemaster class fought with or otherwise supported the Confederacy.

The assassination of President Lincoln was a coup by which a liberal-conservative coalition ushered in a counter-revolution that lasted almost seventy years and reestablished most of the original Liberal Republic. Despite the adoption of the Thirteenth, Fourteenth, and Fifteenth Amendments to the Constitution in 1865–1870 guaranteeing Black rights, reconstruction in the South was aborted by conservative armed forces after Union troops were withdrawn. By 1880, the newly won rights of Blacks had been virtually abolished in the South; genocidal assaults on Native Americans had escalated; the nascent labor movement had been crushed nationwide, and the movement for women's rights had suffered severe setbacks.

This counterrevolution was led by Lincoln's successor, President Andrew Johnson, who narrowly escaped impeachment by the Republican Congress. Although Republican Ulysses S. Grant won the next two presidential elections, progressives were gradually marginalized. The liberal-conservative coalition that had taken power via the 1877 Hayes-Tilden compromise, under which Republican Rutherford B. Hayes had sold out Reconstruction in return for the presidency, was too firmly entrenched to be dislodged by Grant.

From their experience throughout the turbulent but hopeful years of 1790–1880, as well as the following grim years of repression, migration, and depression, Blacks learned that their consistent allies were white progressives and left-wing radicals, the industrial labor movement, and liberal Jews. President Abraham Lincoln became their political icon.

■　■　■

By 1932 America was in a deep economic depression, with tens of millions unemployed or economically deprived and the nation careening toward chaos and armed rebellion. Against this backdrop, Democratic challenger Franklin Delano Roosevelt defeated incumbent Republican President Herbert Hoover by counterposing the New Deal economic renewal to Hoover's policy of doing nothing.

On election day, despite Roosevelt's failure to disown the racist Southern wing of the Democratic Party, Blacks abandoned their traditional support of the Republican Party of Lincoln to join white progressives, working people, and liberals in voting for Roosevelt and his New Deal vision of full employment and an economic safety net for all United States citizens. Thus, a decisive majority of the Black working class and poor chose the temporary priority of economic justice ahead of racial justice.

For the next twelve years, until his death in April of 1945, President Roosevelt's domestic and foreign policies were based on his Four Freedoms—freedom *from* fear, freedom *from* want, freedom *of* speech, and freedom *of* religion. These populist goals helped to spark new mass movements that laid the political, economic, social, and cultural foundations of a twentieth century People's Republic in the tradition of Lincoln's popular government. As in Lincoln's time, the liberal-conservative coalition was swept aside by a progressive-liberal coalition as Roosevelt emerged as a progressive.

The core of his mass support resided in the mushrooming industrial labor movement, led by the Congress of Industrial Organizations (CIO). Millions of Black workers joined the CIO when, unlike its conservative and racist AFL (American Federation of Labor) counterpart, it opened its ranks to all workers without regard to color, creed, or national origin. A powerful coalition of industrial workers and Blacks joined with white progressives and leftists to form a solid progressive political bloc.

With continuously growing popular support for his policies, Roosevelt rebuilt a vibrant industrial economy, united the nation, played a decisive role in winning the global war against the fascist Axis (Nazi Germany, Fascist Italy, and Imperial Japan) as part of the Big Three alliance (the United

States, the Soviet Union, and the United Kingdom), and laid the basis for a lasting world peace anchored by collaboration between the United States, the Soviet Union, Britain, France, and China within the nascent United Nations.

However, on April 12, 1945, three months after his inauguration for a fourth presidential term, President Roosevelt died of a stroke. This was a time when World War II was ending and the process of shaping the peace was at a critical stage. Roosevelt was succeeded by Vice President Harry S Truman of Missouri, a Southern liberal.

Truman immediately revived the traditional liberal-conservative "bipartisan" coalition, cleaned out all progressives from his cabinet and subcabinet, and replaced them with Southern conservatives and Northern liberals. Then he took the fateful step that reversed Roosevelt's foreign policy which was based on postwar collaboration between the United States and the Soviet Union: he ordered the arguably unnecessary atom-bombing of the Japanese cities of Hiroshima and Nagasaki.

This act launched the Cold War, since it was aimed at intimidating the rest of the world with United States military power and not merely at forcing Japan's unconditional surrender. Russia's Premier Joseph Stalin responded by purging the moderates in the Soviet leadership and adopting a hard-line foreign policy designed to challenge and confront the West in his style and on his turf. A year later, Winston Churchill's March 5, 1946, speech at Fulton, Missouri, with President Truman seated on the platform, formally declared the Soviet Union to be the potential enemy of the West. Stalin retaliated in kind.

■　■　■

The Cold War begun by Truman and Stalin in 1946 did not end until 1989, when Soviet President Mikhail Gorbachev unilaterally terminated both the Cold War abroad and Stalinism at home. For forty years following the Soviet Union's testing of its first nuclear weapon in 1949, the entire world had lived in the shadow of nuclear self-destruction.

For Black Americans and the labor movement, the domestic repercussions of Truman's reversal of Roosevelt's foreign policy were immediate and dire. The Truman administration turned a blind eye toward racist repression against returning Black war veterans, which spread throughout the South. Unions found themselves under ferocious attack by employers as well as by the government, as Truman rammed anti-labor legislation through Congress in the name of national security. Civil rights and civil liberties were trampled underfoot by J. Edgar Hoover's Federal Bureau of Investigation, which received license from Truman to ignore constitutional rights in pursuit of vaguely defined Communists and Communist sympathizers.

A coalition of Blacks, labor unions, white progressives and leftists, and liberals with enough courage to defy being labeled unpatriotic mounted a powerful resistance to Truman's domestic policies. By 1948, this movement culminated in the Progressive Party led by Henry Wallace, former vice president during the 1940–1944 wartime Roosevelt administration, which challenged Truman from the left on a platform promising a return to Roosevelt's domestic and foreign policies.

During the 1948 presidential election campaign, the Progressive Party braved Ku Klux Klan intimidation to conduct highly successful voter registration drives throughout the South for the first time since Reconstruction. The AFL, representing labor's conservative wing, remained loyal to Truman and the Democratic Party, along with most liberals and the Black middle-class leadership. The CIO, labor's progressive wing, together with a significant minority of working-class Blacks, white leftists, and a minority of liberals, supported the Progressive Party.

Faced with this challenge from the left, Truman, reversing his domestic course, adopted the domestic platform of the Progressive Party almost in its entirety. Domestically he ran as Roosevelt's heir—the champion of labor and Blacks. He desegregated the armed forces by executive order and similarly enforced fair employment in industry by mandating unbiased hiring at every enterprise that had a government contract. In addition, he issued some important prolabor executive orders, bypassing the antilabor congressional Republicans. Simultaneously, however, he intensified his foreign policy of confrontation with the Soviet Union and its allies. From the foreign-policy standpoint, he ran more against the Soviet leader Stalin than against the heavily favored Republican challenger, New York Governor Thomas E. Dewey.

President Truman's strategy was spectacularly successful. Millions of Blacks and union members who had planned to vote for the Progressive Party switched to Truman, since he had a better chance of winning than Wallace. Many liberals who had defected from the Democratic Party switched back to Truman for the same reason. And a significant number of conservatives decided to vote for Truman because of his tough posture in confronting "world Communism." Contrary to media predictions, Truman was reelected, defeating Dewey in a major upset.

Safely reelected, Truman promptly reversed his domestic course once more. Branding the Progressive Party a tool of the United States Communist Party, he backed the purging of leftists and progressives from the leadership of the labor and civil rights movements and supported a loyalty-oath requirement for public-sector jobs. He sanctioned the indictment, trial, conviction, and long imprisonment of all of the top leaders of the United States Communist Party on the Orwellian charge of "conspiring to teach and advocate the violent overthrow of the U.S. Government." Based on this legal verbiage, political leaders were imprisoned exclusively for their *implicit ideas*, rather than for any *explicit statements* or any *acts*. (Note that "conspiring to teach and advocate" does not even charge that anything at all was ever actually taught or advocated.)

Thus, President Truman's anti-Communist crusade of 1949–1950 laid the foundation for the anti-Communist witch hunt unleashed by the infamous Republican Senator Joseph McCarthy during the early 1950s. By the time the hero-general Dwight D. Eisenhower, a liberal Republican, was elected president in 1952, the world was nearing the threshold of World War III. The United States had intervened militarily in Greece against a Communist-led uprising; North Korea, a Soviet client, had invaded South Korea, a United States client; the United States had intervened in support of South Korea, and China had intervened in support of North Korea and engaged United States troops directly. A military stand-off between the United States and China was temporarily resolved by a shaky truce negotiated through the United Nations.

■ ■ ■

General Eisenhower, a popular war hero, was elected in 1952 in a landslide over the relatively unknown liberal Democratic candidate, Adlai Stevenson. As President, Eisenhower, tend-ing to be more liberal than conservative, strove to achieve domestic tranquility, economic prosperity, and "international peace with honor."

Being a former military man with first-hand experience in war, he pursued a foreign policy based on negotiation and multilateralism in the tradition of Roosevelt, instead of relying upon confrontation and unilateralism as Truman had. In domestic policy, he remained essentially neutral, refusing to back either liberals or conservatives and striving to maintain an even playing field. For example, having inherited a predominantly liberal United States Supreme Court from Truman, he appointed centrists to the Court so that it would remain liberal but less liberal than before.

Consequently, when Stalin died in 1953 and Nikita Khrushchev came to power a year later, President Eisenhower found a willing negotiating partner at the helm of the Soviet Union. By the time Eisenhower left office in 1960, he and Khrushchev had put in place a permanent United States-Soviet negotiation infrastructure.

On the domestic front, white leftists and progressives continued to be driven out of mainstream politics by the extreme right with the consent, or even the participation, of the traditional liberal-conservative coalition. All but an intrepid minority took refuge in the liberal camp. By 1955, the progressive CIO unions had merged with the conservative AFL to form the liberal AFL-CIO. The new organization boasted the all-time high numerical strength of unionized United States workers—35 percent of the total workforce. However, its official program was confined narrowly to strictly union issues, excluding such vital matters as equal rights for Blacks and foreign policy.

The Black working class and white progressives respectively responded by building a mass civil rights movement and a mass peace movement outside of the political mainstream. The Black middle-class leadership and the white liberal leadership opposed these mass movements, but with little success. By 1957, at the beginning of President Eisenhower's second term, the growing civil rights movement led by Rev. Martin Luther King, Jr. was on its way to reviving the Roosevelt coalition of Blacks, progressive labor unions, and white leftists and progressives. By the time of the 1960 presidential elections, the new civil rights movement had attracted most white liberals, forcing both the liberal leadership and the traditional Black leadership to give it at least verbal support.

When liberal Democrat John F. Kennedy was inaugurated following his narrow victory over Vice President Richard Nixon in the 1960 presidential election, he inherited a situation in which he could hope both to end the Cold War and to revive Roosevelt's New Deal at home. He transformed himself into a progressive with the vision and courage to attempt the fulfillment of both tasks. Kennedy outlined the goals of his foreign policy in his inaugural address:

> To those nations who would make themselves our adversary, we offer not a pledge but a request: that both sides begin anew the quest for peace, before the dark powers of destruction unleashed by science engulf all humanity in planned or accidental self-destruction. . . .
>
> . . . Let us begin anew, remembering on both sides that civility is not a sign of weakness, and sincerity is always subject to proof. Let us never negotiate out of fear, but let us never fear to negotiate. . . .
>
> Let both sides unite to heed in all corners of the earth the command of Isaiah to "undo the heavy burdens . . . [and] let the oppressed go free."

This call for a return to Roosevelt's foreign policy was not lost on the Soviet leader, Khrushchev. It helped to provide him with political maneuvering room to risk simultaneous attempts to end the Cold War abroad and launch full de-Stalinization and demilitarization at home. Moreover, it initiated a process in which the two leaders reached a point where they trusted one another sufficiently to wager their political survival on their personal relationship. In my view, this mutual trust prevented a world holocaust during the Cuban missile crisis of 1962 and, ironically, cost Kennedy his physical life in 1963 and Khrushchev his political life in 1964.[2]

Domestically, President Kennedy was the first president to embrace the joint goal of legislating federally enforced civil rights *and* economic rights. On June 11, 1963, as the civil rights movement unfolded and an August civil rights rally promising to bring hundreds of thousands to the capital was being organized, Kennedy declared that Black Americans remained politically, socially, and *economically* oppressed:

> One hundred years of delay have passed since President Lincoln freed the slaves, yet their heirs, their grandsons, are not fully free. They are not yet freed from the bonds of injustice. They are not yet freed from social and economic oppression. . . .
>
> We are confronted primarily with a moral issue. It is as old as the scriptures and is as clear as the American Constitution. The heart of the question is whether all Americans are to be afforded equal rights and equal opportunities. . . . Now the time has come for this nation to fulfill its promise.

This unequivocal challenge to the liberal-conservative coalition's traditional confinement of Black people's rights to a limited part of the political realm while eroding Roosevelt's New Deal asserted Kennedy's shift to a progressive agenda in the teeth of a growing "white backlash." He also made it clear that he would not tolerate anti-Black violence by right-wing extremists, pledging to use the regular army to suppress it, as he had in Mississippi a year earlier. Many liberals opposed this shift, mainly in covert ways. Conservatives were in open political rebellion.

However, the Black working class, especially in the South, was galvanized by President Kennedy's identification with their cause, much as the slaves had been when President Lincoln issued his Emancipation Proclamation. The civil rights movement became an irresistible wave that even Kennedy's assassination five months later could not cause to recede.[3]

History was essentially repeated when Vice President Johnson ascended to the Presidency with an agenda similar to Truman's upon his succession to Roosevelt: the reversal of Kennedy's progressive foreign and domestic policies to satisfy the standard requirements of the traditional liberal-conservative status quo. However, he and the Congress had little choice except to enact comprehensive civil rights legislation. Blacks were now determined to achieve legal equality by compelling the nation to grant it. Moreover, many were prepared to engage in armed conflict if that became necessary to attain equal rights.

The Civil Rights Act was passed in 1965, ushering in a new era in United States history. Like Truman before him, Johnson made major concessions to the progressives' domestic agenda, thus reintegrating them with the liberal wing of the Democratic Party. Having thus neutralized his progressive and leftist opponents, he reversed Kennedy's foreign policy by escalating the Vietnam conflict and confronting the Soviet leadership.

By November of 1964, having contributed significantly to Khrushchev's political overthrow by the neo-Stalinists, Johnson was in a position to coast to reelection on a mixed platform of the "containment of Communism" abroad and the "war on poverty" at home. As Truman had done, he dispersed the progressives, coopted the liberals and the AFL-CIO, bought off the Black middle class, and isolated the Black working class. The winning coalition of Blacks, progressive and leftist whites, and progressive labor had once again been dispersed, and the liberal-conservative status quo was once more in the ascendancy.

■ ■ ■

By the end of 1965, the presidential signing into law of the Civil Rights Act and the Voting Rights Act appeared to have ushered in a new era in United States history—some called it the second Reconstruction. However, this proved to be an illusion. As in Lincoln's and Roosevelt's times, the assassination or untimely death of a progressive president ultimately assured the gradual suppression of a meaningful Reconstruction and the dispersal of the mass movement supporting it. The "new order" was a compromise, and weakly enforced a partial Reconstruction imposed by the perennial liberal-conservative coalition.

In President Kennedy's case, as with President Lincoln, the historical record provides ample evidence that the assassinations were performed by an extreme right-wing faction of the conservative elite. This long-standing group has always maintained a significant presence in the top ranks of the military, intelligence, and executive bureaucracies. It has remained ethnically homogeneous, restricting its leadership almost entirely to Protestant males of English and German descent. A cardinal rule of the traditional liberal-conservative coalition is that this secret center of power shall remain immune from identification, public accountability, or partisan removal from positions of power.[4]

Because of this ethnic imbalance at the power centers of United States society, every United States President save one—John Fitzgerald Kennedy, an Irish Catholic—has been a Protestant male of English or German descent. The only three presidents who have governed as progressives, rather than as representatives of the liberal-conservative coalition, are Lincoln, Roosevelt, and Kennedy. All three died in office under questionable circumstances, which have been covered up by the liberal-conservative coalition but exposed by progressives and leftists.

The seven conspirators who were hanged after being tried for participation in the plot to kill Lincoln apparently had ties to a high-ranking member of United States intelligence, to British intelligence, and at least to one member of the United States Senate. Soviet Premier Stalin stated in a 1945 interview that Soviet intelligence had informed him that President Roosevelt had been poisoned but that no autopsy had been performed. The lack of an autopsy has been confirmed; the poisoning has not. Concerning the Kennedy assassination, abundant evidence has been published to support both sides of the ongoing debate as to whether there was a conspiracy or not.[5]

President Kennedy's plans for his second term have been discussed in considerable detail, notably by Robert Dallek in a piece titled, "JFK's Second Term," appearing in the June 2003 issue of *The Atlantic Monthly*. Dallek confirms that Kennedy intended to dismantle completely the right-wing's secret infrastructure in the executive branch, beginning with the military and intelligence departments. Moreover, mindful of departing President Eisenhower's criticism of the military-industrial complex, Kennedy was determined to curb its power.

The warmongering attitude of the Joint Chiefs of Staff, especially their readiness to resort to nuclear weapons in any and every situation in which conventional forces could not win quickly and with minimal losses, appalled him. Apparently, he resolved to remove them as a group during his second term. Dallek writes:

> Shortly after the [1961] Bay of Pigs debacle, . . . the Joint Chiefs urged Kennedy to authorize the use of air and land forces in Laos to avert a communist takeover. Kennedy wanted to know what they intended if such an operation failed. The Joint Chiefs answered, in the words of Attorney General Robert F. Kennedy, "You start using atomic weapons!" Lyman Lemnitzer, the Chairman of the Joint Chiefs, promised that if they were given authorization to use nuclear weapons, they could guarantee victory. Kennedy saw Lemnitzer's assurance as absurd. . . . Kennedy felt the most tension with General Lauris Norstad, the commander of NATO forces, and General Curtis LeMay, the chief of staff of the Air Force. Both Norstad and LeMay believed that any war with the Soviet Union would have to escalate quickly into a nuclear exchange if the United States was to have any hope of "winning." Kennedy found LeMay, who would become the model for a deranged general in the 1964 movie *Dr. Strangelove*, especially intolerable.[6]

Today, military and intelligence officials such as Kennedy's joint chiefs, as well as their civilian allies, are called "neocons" by liberals, "extreme conservatives" by mainstream conservatives, "ultrarightists" by progressives, "racists" by Blacks, and "fascists" by leftists. During the Kennedy presidency, liberals, who had been in power since 1932, removed the extreme conservatives from high governmental positions whenever they could do so under "bipartisan" rules.

On the other hand, conservatives remained allied with ultraconservatives, shielding the most extreme ones from exposure or attack as a group. Whenever the conservative wing was dominant, it placed a few ultraconservatives in high government positions.

The bipartisan rules governing congressional political conflict resemble those of a private club or fraternity and are generally practiced faithfully by all elected members of government with minor variations according to party affiliation. Breaches of the rules are adjudicated by bipartisan internal "ethics" committees whose proceedings are secret.

Tradition commands that no elected official shall be placed within the jurisdiction of the judicial branch of government by the other branches, *unless it can be proven in court that this person has broken the law.* Even then, an "independent" special prosecutor approved by the legislative branch must recommend a criminal indictment by a grand jury before any judicial action can proceed. Thus, the entrenched United States "two-party system" automatically creates a *self-perpetuating political class.*

The thirty-six-year period 1932–1968 was dominated politically by two progressive presidents (Roosevelt and Kennedy), who governed for a total of fifteen years, and three liberal presidents (Truman, Eisenhower, and Johnson), who governed for a total of twenty-one years. Consequently, at the end of this period, liberals were overwhelmingly dominant, whereas virtually all progressives and ultraconservatives were gone.

Although Roosevelt and Kennedy had managed to appoint a large number of progressives during their combined fifteen years in office, the partisan liberals Truman and Johnson had weeded out most of them during their combined thirteen-year tenure. Centrist liberal Eisenhower simply didn't reappoint most of the remaining ones during his eight years in the White House.

Ultraconservatives fared no better than progressives. Eisenhower tended to appoint conservatives while ignoring ultraconservatives, and all four Democratic presidents removed many. Consequently, by the time Johnson left office in 1968, the two-party system was unusually stable under the guiding hand of a virtually all-powerful bipartisan coalition of liberals and conservatives. With both the right and the left eliminated as organized groups, the government was overwhelmingly centrist.

Blacks had not fared well during Johnson's two terms. Two assassinations had decapitated the Black leadership: Malcolm X had been gunned down in 1964 while speaking in Harlem's Audubon Ballroom, and Rev. Martin Luther King, Jr. had been murdered by a sniper in 1968 on the balcony of a motel room in Memphis, Tennessee. The top labor leadership under George Meany, President of the AFL-CIO, was safely under the political sway of the liberal wing of the Democratic Party and had been purged of leftists, progressives, and independent Black union leaders. The Black caucuses in most of the AFL-CIO local unions had been driven underground.

The Black poor, inspired by the civil rights movement, were bypassed by its results. Civil rights did not bring jobs, education, or even sustained hope. During the period 1965–1968, the anguished cry of the impoverished ghetto masses rang out across the nation as their rebellious fury looted and burned stores and other commercial enterprises in the Black neighborhoods and downtown areas of a hundred cities. More than 200 people died, and over 4,000 were wounded. In five days, July 23–27, 1967, the Detroit riot left 43 dead, 1,200 injured, 7,231 arrested, 5,000 homeless, and over 1,300 buildings destroyed.

In many cities, spontaneous armed-gang resistance drove out the local police and even the state police when they attempted to enter the Black ghettos. In the end, only National Guard units, backed up by regular army detachments with tanks, were able to establish law and order fully. The civil rights leadership was ineffectual to the point of helplessness.

Conservatives and ultraconservatives demanded a military solution consisting of ghetto pacification by overwhelming armed force that would establish a police state inside the ghettos. One National Guard general who advocated the use of artillery was promptly reassigned by his superiors, but military contingency plans were prepared.

After rioting in Black communities erupted again following the assassination of Rev. Martin Luther King, Jr., on April 4, 1968, the House Committee on Un-American Activities under the chairmanship of Edwin E. Willis, a Louisiana Democrat, sent a report to President Johnson on May 6. Titled, *Guerilla Warfare Advocates in the United States*, the report included a plan to "seal off" Black ghettos from the rest of the city by deploying police backed up by the National Guard and regular-army troops. Then police-state regulations would be enforced, including a curfew and military law.

Johnson rejected the report out of hand, and managed to institutionalize the War on Poverty before he left office.

In 1968, the assassination of Robert F. Kennedy, the progressive front runner poised to become the 1968 Democratic presidential nominee, further weakened the progressives. After the Democratic convention, the compromise nominee, Hubert Humphrey, found himself at a disadvantage because he had alienated progressives by dropping all of their demands from his platform. Early September polls showed him losing to Nixon in a landslide. Only then did he switch gears and adopt the progressive platform, including a pledge to end the Vietnam War. However, his move came too late. He lost to Nixon by less than 1 percent.

The elimination of Bobby Kennedy, King, and Malcolm weakened the progressives' Black political base and split the Democratic Party, contributing greatly to ultraconservative Nixon's victory. Although Nixon was an avowed ultraconservative, he campaigned successfully as a centrist in order to appeal to the centrist mood of a nation exhausted by the trauma of the civil rights revolution. This transformation was probably behind the political epithet "tricky Dick" that became associated with him.

Once elected, he revealed his true political allegiances by making wholesale appointments of ultraconservatives throughout the government infrastructure. At the same time, he strove to expand his presidential powers beyond their constitutional limits. These combined actions led leftists, progressives, and even some liberals to characterize his presidency as corrupt and imperial. Ultimately, Nixon's persistence in such political behavior led to the Watergate scandal and an alleged attempt at a presidential coup.[7]

The resulting national crisis was resolved only when Nixon was compelled to resign in the wake of the bipartisan approval of three articles of impeachment by the United States House of Representatives.

■ ■ ■

Vice President Gerald Ford was a bland mainstream conservative who resembled Eisenhower rather than Nixon. Moreover, he was far too ordinary a figure to have been able to pursue Nixon's agenda, even had he wished to. Having no discernible vision, he sought stability and conflict resolution. He left the administrative bureaucracy he inherited in place and pacified Nixon's constituency by immediately issuing Nixon a pardon. To pacify liberals and Blacks, he chose New York Governor Nelson Rockefeller as his vice president. As a result of these maneuvers, Blacks, progressives, and labor were further marginalized politically, and the Cold War ground on as it had since 1945 but in a far more manageable and institutionalized form.

In 1976, the southern Democrat Jimmy Carter, running as a liberal update of Presidents Truman and Johnson, easily turned back Ted Kennedy, his progressive challenger at the Democratic Party convention and went on to defeat Ford in the presidential election. Carter continued Ford's basic centrist foreign and domestic policies and consolidated the liberal dominance within the liberal-conservative "bipartisan" coalition at the expense of the ultraconservatives and progressives. He achieved a significant rise in general prosperity, including major gains in employment and at least marginal gains for Blacks and labor. However, much of the middle class was alienated by the rise of inflation that accompanied his pro–working class economic initiatives.

This was the context in which the ultraconservatives launched their "Reagan Revolution" in 1980. Ronald Reagan, a former B-movie actor turned politician, had won the California governorship as an ultraconservative. At the 1980 Republican Convention, the ultraconservatives saw in Reagan an opportunity to seize control of the Republican Party and to return to presidential power after a forty-eight-year exile. With united ultraconservative and conservative backing, Reagan won the Republican nomination.

During the 1980 presidential campaign, Carter, true to the liberal tradition, tried unsuccessfully to compete with Reagan's fiscally conservative message in order to win over middle-class voters. In doing so, he abandoned the interests of the Democratic Party's natural base of labor, Blacks, and progressives. Worse, he altered his economic policies to accommodate middle-class priorities, thereby eroding working-class gains *and* fueling inflation. He was still in a position to defeat Reagan until independent candidate John Anderson mounted a campaign on behalf of the disaffected middle class.

Faced with certain defeat, Carter finally went back to his base in the style of Truman, Johnson, and Humphrey. However, as in Humphrey's case, it was probably too late. Even so, he still had a chance to win when it appeared that he had negotiated a deal with Iran's new fundamentalist ruler, Ayatollah Ruhollah Khomeini, to return American hostages held in the wake of Carter's disastrously aborted "desert raid" against Iran.

Several unverified reports have provided significant (but not completely verified) evidence implying that, in direct contravention of United States Federal law, several anonymous ultraconservatives close to Reagan successfully negotiated with Iran's leader, Ayatollah Khomeini, to withhold release of the hostages until after the election, in return for arms if Reagan was elected to the presidency. Denied the triumphal return of the hostages on the eve of the election, Carter had no chance, and Reagan won a landslide electoral college victory. However, the popular vote was far closer, with Reagan capturing just under 51 percent. Without Anderson in the race, and aided by a return of the hostages by Iran, Carter may well have won.

Thus was the arms-for-hostages "Irangate" scandal born. Regrettably, the mainstream media tended to trivialize the depth of this scandal, persistently failing to connect the dots between the illegal exchange of arms for hostages, the alleged illegal preelection negotiations with Ayatollah Khomeini, and the verified illegal exchange of cocaine shipments for arms shipments to the Nicaraguan Contras.

Consequently, a second conspiracy of sorts became acceptable—a conspiracy of media silence. To me, the phrase "speaking truth to power" means breaking this silence. Moreover, "leaders" are supposed to do this as a matter of principle.

The "Reagan Revolution" began with Reagan's inauguration as the fortieth United States president in January, 1981.

Domestically, he created the greatest deficit in modern United States history (with the possible exception of President George W. Bush, who has not yet completed his second term in office). Several impartial observers, as well as Reagan's former Budget Director, John Stockman, have expressed the view that Reagan did so intentionally, in order to starve the treasury to the point where significant levels of public social spending would be impossible.

Whether or not this was the case, Reagan's across-the-board attack against all economic policies derived from Roosevelt's New Deal has been thoroughly documented. Deregulation benefiting large corporations was instituted;

labor unions were placed at the mercy of state legislatures, and ultraconservative nominees to the United States Supreme Court were submitted with a view toward rolling back pro-Black and prolabor legislation and upholding states' rights.

Reagan left a substantial record of revealing quotes during the decade preceding his tenure as Governor of California and as President of the United States.[8]

In the sphere of ideology, he defamed the Roosevelt legacy by labeling it "fascist" and misrepresenting its aims:

> Fascism was really the basis for the New Deal. . . . Anyone who wants to take a look at the writings of the members of the brain trust of the New Deal will find that President Roosevelt's advisers admired the fascist system. . . . Many of the New Dealers actually espoused what has become an epithet—fascism. . . . Ickes, Harold Ickes [Roosevelt's Secretary of the Interior], in his book, said what we were striving for was a kind of modified form of communism.

In 1980, he chose to kick off his presidential campaign in Philadelphia, Mississippi, site of the 1964 torture and murder of three young civil rights workers, with a speech supporting states' rights. Soon thereafter, he refused to decline the support of the Ku Klux Klan. These acts alone are sufficient to call President Ronald Reagan the most openly racist politician who has run for the highest office on a major-party ticket since World War I.

With regard to religion, Reagan identified himself as a "born-again" Christian (as distinct from a Judeo-Christian), and embraced the extreme fundamentalist concept of Armageddon, or the world apocalypse, in which only "pure" Christians survive.

This is the overall political profile of America's original "compassionate conservative"—Good old Ronnie, whose style endeared him to a majority of white Americans. When he ran for reelection in 1984, white voters chose him over Democrat Walter Mondale by 64 percent to 35 percent. In stark contrast, Black voters chose Mondale over Reagan by 90 percent to 9 percent. Since the vast majority of Black Americans were concerned primarily with substance and issues, they were not distracted from their interests by the candidates' personality or style. They recognized Ronald Reagan for what he was—the faithful political servant of the heirs of the slave-owning South.

Blacks had been galvanized by Rev. Jesse Jackson's historic campaign for the Democratic Party's presidential nomination. Having entered the race against the opposition of virtually the entire civil rights leadership, he won 21 percent of the vote in the primaries and caucuses by building a strong nationwide progressive coalition based on an undiluted progressive platform. Although the Democratic convention rejected both his platform and his candidacy, he had sown the seeds of a Black political renaissance.

By 1986, Black voters were already organizing nationwide to support Rev. Jesse Jackson's second run for the United States presidency. They joined their main allies—labor, progressives, and leftists—to bring the Reagan political juggernaut to a halt by anchoring a major Republican defeat in the 1986 midterm congressional elections. The revived power of the Democratic Party in Congress grew with the approach of the 1988 presidential election, as the continued momentum of Jackson's 1984 presidential run among Black voters merged with a progressive revival in the unions and on the college campuses.

By 1988, the negative domestic results of Reagan's economic policies and the lingering damage inflicted on his administration by the Irangate scandal had weakened his presidency to the point where the Democrats could override his veto of a civil rights bill and prevent his termination of affirmative action by executive order.

In foreign policy, the stated Reagan aim had been to "win" the Cold War at all costs by forcing the complete collapse of the Soviet Union, renamed the "evil empire," by means of a relentless application of military pressure, subversion, and economic pressure. But by the end of Reagan's second term, this policy was in shambles, reduced essentially to improvised adjustments to an unending series of Russian initiatives.

Beginning with Mikhail Gorbachev's 1985 ascent to full political power in the Soviet Union, Reagan's foreign policy collided with the unfolding Gorbachev Revolution that ultimately led to dissolution of the Soviet Union in 1991. Gorbachev and his supporters were true to their word. By 1990, only five years later, they had dismantled both Stalinism and Leninism as guiding state ideologies and returned to the ideological realm of Marx and Engels.

In the political sphere, they had achieved a mixture of parliamentary and republican democracy, undermining the power of the Communist Party to the point where it could no longer govern without the consent of the people, and a multiparty system was already rising within the party itself.

In the economic realm, a mixed economy was developing with the goal of stable social democracy and a powerful public sector.

In the cultural/social area, every Soviet republic except Lithuania had supported the "Gorbachev referendum" by more than a two-thirds vote. Gorbachev's new draft constitution for what was nominally a "socialist union" but actually a socialist confederacy guaranteed the Republics the right to secede.

Gorbachev radically revised traditional Soviet foreign policy principles. *Human* priorities were declared to transcend *class* priorities. This ideological leap carried the Gorbachev leadership beyond the constraints of Marxist principles into the sphere of Social Democratic thought. On a world scale, Gorbachev embraced the vision of world government via an empowered United Nations, an update of President Kennedy's idea expressed briefly in his 1961 Inaugural Address.

He carried out *unilateral* partial demilitarization and disarmament under his new doctrine of *deterrent sufficiency,* which replaced the Brezhnev doctrine of *military parity*. This provided Gorbachev with a wide negotiating range between the existing military overkill concealed in the phrase "military parity" and the far lower level required by deterrent sufficiency. Thus armed, he continually made so many incremental concessions that Reagan could not say no. As a result, Gorbachev succeeded in unilaterally causing a reversal of the entire Cold War environment by the end of Reagan's second term in 1988. The Gorbachev revolution had, in Gorbachev's words, "taken away America's enemy." It had also taken away the ultraconservatives' chief weapon: fear.

Gorbachev visited all of the Soviet Union's Eastern European Warsaw Pact allies personally, stating publicly that every country's national sovereignty had priority over "international socialist solidarity." He also made it clear publicly that Soviet troops stationed in the Warsaw Pact countries would not intervene to support any attempts by individual governments to repress their own people.

By this time, Gorbachev's visit to the United States and Reagan's visit to Russia, followed by a stream of exchange visits by Americans and Russians on all levels, had demolished, at least temporarily, the Cold War stereotypes and perceptions that had been implanted in the minds of both the American and Russian people by over forty years of propaganda. The gregarious and engaging personalities of the leaders played a decisive role in accelerating this process. In this international environment, the entire ultraconservative foreign policy agenda became obsolete.

Gorbachev ordered Soviet troops stationed in both Czechoslovakia and East Germany under the Warsaw Pact to prevent the Czech and East German military from suppressing peaceful mass demonstrations. A year later, in 1989, when peaceful mass demonstrations overthrew the Communist governments of Poland, Czechoslovakia, Hungary and East Germany by forcing free elections or by forced resignations, Gorbachev ordered Soviet troops stationed in those countries to prevent the military suppression of the popular rebellions.

When West German youth began tearing down the Berlin Wall on November 11, 1989, most of the East German border guards looked on passively. A few joined in to help dismantle it from their side. As the wall came tumbling down, it both ended the Cold War and marked the beginning of the end of the Reagan revolution.

But Gorbachev could hardly be called a winner. He had "lost" Eastern Europe; the Warsaw alliance was dead, and Soviet troops had withdrawn behind Soviet borders. Worse still, his domestic policies had produced a state of perpetual crisis. Revolutionary processes, even the slow and relatively controlled one that Gorbachev had unleashed, are risky and messy at best. At worst, they end in civil war. It is a tribute to Gorbachev's extraordinary political skills and his sheer will that his revolution did not spin out of control. His fragile domestic position placed him at a huge disadvantage when he faced the newly elected Republican President George H.W. Bush in 1989. Bush, a centrist more in the mold of President Ford than of President Reagan, presented Gorbachev with an unfamiliar challenge.

■ ■ ■

The 1988 presidential election story featured Rev. Jesse Jackson's second run for the United States presidency as a progressive Democrat. This time, he won 27 percent of the vote in the Democratic primaries and caucuses—enough to pose a serious challenge to the liberal front runner, Massachusetts Governor Michael Dukakis. The liberal Democratic leadership closed ranks behind Dukakis, and as in 1984, the convention rejected Jackson's nomination bid and his progressive message. Dukakis won the nomination and campaigned on a cautiously liberal platform.

At the beginning of the campaign, Dukakis, enjoying a seventeen-point lead, focused almost exclusively on winning over middle-class swing voters while virtually ignoring the Democratic base of Blacks, white progressives, and other minorities. By contrast, the Republican Party machine ran one of the dirtiest campaigns in modern history, race-baiting and red-baiting Dukakis with an abandon not seen since the Orwellian days of the anti-Communist witch hunt of the 1950s.

Dukakis remained on the defensive, failing to hold Bush publicly accountable for the Republican campaign ads. He refused to attack their racist content or to counter Bush's Cold War demagogy about Democrats being "soft" on the "Communist threat" by exposing Bush's false foreign policy premises. As a result, he lost to Bush by a popular-vote margin of 53 to 45 percent and an electoral defeat by 426 to 111. Dukakis's lackluster campaign was the main reason for the lowest voter turnout since 1924.

Nevertheless, the Black-labor progressive base of the Democratic Party won enough congressional seats to prevent the Bush administration from returning to Reagan's discredited domestic and foreign policies. Despite Bush's preelection promise to adhere to ultraconservative domestic and foreign policies, even his own conservative-dominated administration obstructed his pursuit of such a course. Chairman of the Joint Chiefs of Staff Colin Powell, the only Republican liberal in the administration, joined with conservatives Brent Scowcroft, Bush's National Security Adviser, and Secretary of State James Baker to neutralize the ultraconservatives led by Secretary of Defense Richard Cheney.

Moreover, it was Powell whose private briefing of President Bush influenced him to end the first Persian Gulf War with a cease-fire, stopping short of a march to Baghdad to overthrow Saddam Hussein. Since the political and military goals established by the international coalition Bush had built had been accomplished, Powell argued, he and field commander General Norman Schwartzkopf were recommending an immediate cease-fire. Bush made up his mind to end the war on the basis of Powell's briefing, and the subsequent war-cabinet meeting rubber-stamped his decision.[9]

By guaranteeing that the United States did not march to Baghdad, as the ultraconservatives, some conservatives, and even some liberal Democrats would have liked, Colin Powell almost certainly prevented the resumption of a full-blown cold war and an abrupt reversal of the accelerating trend toward nuclear disarmament. Gorbachev, in two historic March 1991 speeches delivered a few days apart in Minsk, had issued blunt public warnings to Bush that a United States-imposed "regime change" in Iraq meant that all bets were off between the United States and Russia.

It appears that Powell, an astute diplomat who had taken the trouble to familiarize himself thoroughly with the Soviet political and military cultures and to cultivate sustained personal relations with the top Soviet military leaders, immediately recognized the peril and acted swiftly and decisively to negotiate a cease fire. Thus, he headed off a major international crisis, and saved the SALT treaties limiting nuclear arms and the Anti-Ballistic-Missile Treaty which he, more than any other United States negotiator, had guided to adoption. Little did he know then that an abortive coup would cause the collapse of the Soviet Union five months later.[10]

As the renominated Bush-Quayle Republican ticket began the 1992 presidential campaign against the rival Clinton-Gore ticket, an independent third-party ticket headed by Ross Perot doomed Bush's reelection chances. Perot's poll numbers were in the low teens and climbing, with most of his support coming from disenchanted Republicans. With the economy still unrecovered from Reagan's near-demolition of it and Bush's inability to articulate a coherent economic policy, Clinton's unmatched skills as a political campaigner gave him a significant advantage.

When the 1992 presidential votes had been counted, Clinton had won by 43 percent to 38 percent, with Ross Perot's third-party ticket drawing 19 percent. Perot's candidacy, rather than Clinton's platform or personality, defeated Bush. Perot received 20 percent of the white vote, reducing Bush's 1988 white vote from 59 percent to only 40 percent. Clinton received 39 percent of the white vote—a figure 1 percent lower than Dukasis's 40 percent in 1988 and 8 percent lower than Carter's in 1976. Moreover, Clinton's 83 percent of the Black vote was 3 percent lower than Dukakis's 1988 figure and 7 percent lower than Mondale's 90 percent in 1984.

The reason for Clinton's lower white vote was his lack of any progressive elements in his campaign platform. His lower Black vote was caused by the absence of a strong Black contender, such as Jesse Jackson in 1984 and 1988, from the Democratic primary campaign. This implies that, contrary to conventional wisdom, a visibly powerful Black presence in the Democratic Party and a *liberal-progressive* platform (as distinct from an *exclusively liberal* one) increases both white and Black votes for Democrats.

Thus, it appears that the majority of both white and Black Americans want a liberal-progressive government instead of a liberal-conservative one. In other words, the present political crisis apparently stems from the unsuccessful imposition of a liberal-conservative status quo on a society that requires a liberal-progressive system. Consequently, *center-right* political power is being challenged by a *center-left* opposition.

The 1992 election of the Clinton-Gore Democratic ticket signaled the end of the Reagan revolution and coincided with the onset of the "digital revolution." Clinton came to the presidency with the objective of temporarily stabilizing the center-right political system by finding a "third way."

Recognizing, I believe correctly, that the conventional "right" and "left" political options have been rendered obsolete by historical events, Clinton set out to shift the present United States center-right system to a center-left system by means of skillful political manipulations. Regrettably, these means were inadequate. Traversing a political arc similar to Gorbachev's in the former Soviet Union, he succeeded in undermining the existing system he tried to reform from within but failed to create a durable base for the new one.

Consequently, it appears to me that one cannot *reform* a political *system*; one can only overthrow it and replace it with a new one. The process is called a *revolution* for the very reason that it cannot be accomplished by *reform*.

In the past, revolutions, whether successful or failed, have always been violent, although to vastly different degrees. Consequently, it is entirely unrealistic to believe that a revolution in the present or future can be *completely* nonviolent. Nevertheless, the experience of the civil rights revolution justifies the strong hope that a revolution on an even greater scale is achievable with a minimum of violence if it unfolds gradually, in stages.

Since it appears that such a social revolution has already begun to unfold on a world scale, as well as in the United States, it behooves all Americans to find the political will to fashion the political tools required to meet its challenges in a peaceful way. The alternative facing us and the entire world is chaos, death, and destruction on a scale dwarfing World War II and its aftermath.

For we shall live or perish together as a single human family. In the terrain we have entered and from which we cannot escape, there is no third way.

NOTES

1. Philip A. Klinkner with Rogers M. Smith, *The Unsteady March*, Chicago and London; University of Chicago Press, 1999. See also: James M. McPherson, *Abraham Lincoln and the Second American Revolution*, New York and Oxford; Oxford University Press, 1991; Benjamin Quarles, *Lincoln and the Negro*, New York; Da Capo Press,1990.

2. Kennedy and Khrushchev negotiated an end to the Cuban missile crisis secretly, excluding everyone else except one trusted aide on each side. Attorney General Robert Kennedy, JFK's brother, served President Kennedy, and Soviet Ambassador to the U.S., Anatoly Dobrynin, served Khrushchev.

Kennedy had decided to expel ultraconservatives from positions of power within the military and intelligence communities after the Bay of Pigs disaster, while Khrushchev had already begun to remove the Stalinist counterpart to the United States ultraright in 1956 in the wake of his famous "secret speech" denouncing Stalin's crimes.

The resolution of the Cuban missile crisis by the *progressive* Kennedy and the *Leninist reformer* Khrushchev signaled the beginning of the end of the Cold War and the demilitarization of both the United States and the Soviet Union.

However, by 1964, the ultraright had assassinated Kennedy on behalf of the Southern WASP faction of the United States military-industrial complex, and Khrushchev had been overthrown by a coup perpetrated by the Soviet neo-Stalinist counterpart of the United States ultraright. It was led by Khrushchev's own appointee heading the KGB (the Soviet counterpart of the combined CIA, FBI and Department of Defense Intelligence).

Kennedy had not been able to demilitarize the United States during his slightly less than three years in office, just as Lincoln, during his slightly more than four years in office, had not been able to put in place the *personnel* (especially a Congress) capable of seeing Reconstruction through to the end.

Khrushchev was succeeded by Leonid Brezhnev, a shrewd but undereducated party hack who functioned politically as an ultracautious centrist. He found a perfect partner in President Lyndon Johnson, a flamboyant figure who functioned politically as an ultracautious centrist.

The mixed consequences of their partnership was the failure of the United States to demilitarize, the remilitarization of the Soviet Union in a modernized mode, and the institutionalized management of the Cold War in a manner that has successfully avoided *any* direct United States-Soviet military confrontation at *any* level.

The ever more deadly long-term result of this status quo has been a permanent great-powers arms race with ever wider proliferation of nuclear weapons; the spread of regional wars; the growing impoverishment of three-quarters of the world's population; the rapid deterioration of the world's environment; and the exponentially rising spread of terrorism.

3. I believe that by 1965, an unknown but significant number of Black Americans were determined to use *any means necessary* to claim, take, and hold the civil rights guaranteed to every United States citizen by the United States Constitution. In the deep South, armed rebellion on a scale requiring massive federal military intervention would have been a certainty.

4. In general, such groups are variously identified by the familiar phrases, "mob syndicate," "industrial syndicate," "banking syndicate," "Opus Dei," "the Muslim Brotherhood," "the Masons," "the Klan," the Russian "Black Hundreds," the Chinese "Tong Syndicate." A few modern United States phrases referring to a group of this kind are, Eisenhower's "military-industrial complex," or Bill and Hillary Clinton's "right-wing conspiracy."

5. Some of the main arguments supporting the conspiracy-theory position are the following:

During the time frame within which Kennedy could have been a target, the rifle used by the alleged assassin Oswald could not have fired the four recorded shots. The Warren Commission concluded, falsely, that there were only three shots.

The laws of physics dictate that the one recovered bullet allegedly wounding both Kennedy and Governor Connally could not possibly have traveled along the required trajectory or inflicted the amount of bone damage that Connally suffered. A second bullet, never recovered, must have been fired to inflict such extensive physical damage. The Warren Commission came to the false conclusion that there could have been only one bullet.

The shot to the head that killed Kennedy came from the grassy knoll in front of him, as confirmed by the initial backward snap of his head clearly visible on the videotape of the assassination. The Warren Commission asserted that the shot must have come from behind Kennedy.

The Dallas hospital doctors who treated Kennedy reported a small entry wound in the forehead and a large exit wound at the rear of the skull, confirming that the head shot must have been fired from the front. Kennedy's skull and brain apparently vanished after the official autopsy was performed.

There were two different "Oswalds," one of whom may have had ties to both the CIA and the Field Operations Unit of United States Army Intelligence.

6. The movie was not entirely a fantasy. On at least one occasion, a United States strategic bomber went beyond the "fail-safe" boundary. Fortunately it was recalled just in time, and the Soviet military did not react according to the "book" but according to common sense. It was also true that Khrushchev had ordered the successful production of an estimated four "Strangelove" superbombs with operational delivery systems—*100*

megaton "continent busters." These immense hydrogen bombs were *one thousand times* more powerful than the 50-kiloton atomic bombs that destroyed Hiroshima and Nagasaki. They could be used only defensively, in response to a "first strike."

7. The coup danger was indirectly referred to by Sam Ervin, Democratic Senator from North Carolina and chairman of the Senate committee investigating Watergate, who commented that the Nixon administration had a "Gestapo mentality." General Alexander Haig, a top Nixon aide, was addressing rumors about a planned presidential military coup when he called the Watergate period "the most dangerous in American history" in his 1979 memoir. Nixon's Secretary of Defense, James Schlesinger, apparently had the same danger in mind when he told the Joint Chiefs of Staff that all orders to the military from the White House must be referred to him. And Republican Senator Lowell Weiker of Connecticut termed Watergate a scheme by some "to steal America."

8. The following quotes are representative. [See: Mark Green & Gail Mac-Coll, *Ronald Reagan's Reign of Error*, New York; Pantheon Books, 1983.]

> Fascism is private ownership, private enterprise, but [with] total government control and regulation. Well, isn't this the liberal philosophy? [*Newsweek*, January 12, 1976].

> This whole progressive tax system is a foreign import spawned by Karl Marx a century ago. . . . [*Screen Actor*, September 1979]

> Unemployment insurance is a prepaid vacation for freeloaders. . . . [*Sacramento Bee*, April 28, 1966].

> Take the war on poverty—a matchless boondoggle, full of sound and fury, but still with no record of accomplishment. . . . [Speech before the Merchants and Manufacturers Association, May 16, 1966].

> We were told . . . that 17 million people went to bed hungry every night. Well, that was because they were all on a diet. . . . [TV Speech, October 27, 1964].

> [Medicaid recipients are] a faceless mass, waiting for handouts. . . . [1965]

> It doesn't do any good to open doors for someone who doesn't have the price to get in; if he has the price, he may not need the laws. . . . There is no law saying the Negro has to live in Harlem or Watts [*San Francisco Chronicle*, September 9, 1967].

I would have voted against the Civil Rights Act of 1964 [*Los Angeles Times*, June 17, 1966].

9. On this and other matters concerning the role of Colin Powell in the Reagan, G. H. W. Bush, Clinton, and G. W. Bush administrations, as well as his personal history, see: Colin L. Powell with Joseph Persico, *My American Journey*, New York, Random House, 1995; Bob Woodward, *The Commanders*, New York, Simon & Schuster, 1991; Bob Woodward, *Bush At War*, New York, Simon & Schuster, 2002; Bob Woodward, *Plan of Attack*, New York, Simon & Schuster, 2004; Richard Clarke, *Against All Enemies*, New York, Free Press, 2004.

10. Concerning Gorbachev, see his memoirs [*Memoirs*, Doubleday, 1996], as well as the memoirs of Boris Yeltsin [*Against the Grain*, Simon and Schuster, 1995; *The Struggle for Russia*, Crown, 1994]. With regard to the 1991 "August Coup," see General Alexander Lebed's memoir [*My Life and My Country*, National Book Network, 1997] and the memoir of Jack Matlock Jr., President G. H. W. Bush's ambassador to Moscow [*Autopsy on an Empire*, Random House, 1995; *Reagan and Gorbachev*, Random House, 2005].

Gorbachev opposed both the democratic reformers, who wanted to establish a Western-style liberal democracy with a free-market economy, and the right-wing Russian nationalists. His unrealistic vision was a confederated union of autonomous republics, which was committed to social democracy, a mixed economy, and the "socialist idea."

He was aware of the perfidy of some of his close associates, including the coup leaders Dmitri Yazov (the defense minister), Ivan Pavlov (the prime minister), Vladimir Kryuchkov (the head of the KGB), Gennady Yanaev (the vice president), and Anatoly Lukyanov (the chairman of Parliament). He did not act, he writes, because he believed, correctly, that he had already lost real power. Consequently, his only strength was to refrain from action, thus forcing any coup to act illegally against the popularly elected Parliament and its President.

Even though he grasped the nature and popularity of nationalist aspirations in the republics, he could not overcome the unholy alliance of radical democrats and extreme nationalists, led by Yeltsin, that deliberately destroyed the Soviet Union in order to take power in Russia.

Former Ambassador Matlock reveals that Bush cut a secret deal with Yeltsin to help him gain power in Russia at Gorbachev's expense after a coup that was guaranteed to fail by virtue of Yeltsin's secret deal with the paratroop general who commanded the troops in the Moscow district. General Alexander Lebed, the deputy commander of the troops controlling Moscow during the coup, exposes its phony nature.

The radical democrat Gavril Popov, then the Mayor of Moscow, sent a warning about the coup to Yeltsin in Washington, D.C., via United States Ambassador Matlock instead of warning Gorbachev. Yeltsin then agreed that President Bush should call Gorbachev on the hot line to warn him about the impending coup, naming the coup plotters.

It is not surprising that this sequence of events triggered the coup, since there can be little doubt that Kryuchkov, the head of the KGB, was listening in. Popov himself, in a 1992 article titled "August Ninety-One"(*Izvestiya*, August 21–24, 1992), indirectly confirms this plot:

> A collision was inevitable. This was understood by both democrats and conservatives. . . . The conservatives understood that in the fall we would be the ones to give battle. . . . We couldn't wait any longer. The people were demanding reforms from us, and we had a duty to begin them, having taken away the right of the center to interfere in the affairs of Russia. . . . The G.Ch.K.P [the committee set up by the putschists] was, of course, a violation of law. But we too would have had to violate it (as, by the way, things occurred when the USSR was liquidated). . . .
>
> . . . The most favorable variant for us was a putsch "against Gorbachev.". . . Of all the possible [putsch] variants, the . . . plotters chose one we could only dream about: not merely against Gorbachev but also with his isolation. . . .

The reason the United States aid to Gorbachev was infinitesimal compared to the aid lavished on Yeltsin resides in Gorbachev's blunt warning to the West: "No foreigners are going to control us with their money; we may be poor, but we're proud and independent." Moreover, Gorbachev, like the vast majority of the Russian electorate, was categorically opposed to the free market. It is high time that United States policy makers accepted the unalterable fact that the free market is dead in Russia and cannot be resurrected except by violent authoritarian means.

Moreover, Gorbachev, in a *New York Times* op-ed piece appearing on February 10, 1996, asserted that "some in the West have attempted ruthlessly to exploit the strains and weaknesses in Russian policy." He added that Russians see the plan to expand NATO eastward " as something that didn't change with the end of the cold war—as a war machine that is trying to take advantage of our troubled political and economic situation." Finally, he warned of "a real danger that we'll restart the arms race." In my view, he was responding, in part, to the incessant United

States claim that America won the Cold War and is now the world's sole superpower.

Yeltsin, now derisively referred to by many Russians as "Tsar Boris," was an opportunistic political thug who hijacked Russia and stole her nearly blind. The G. H. W. Bush and Clinton administrations mistakenly believed that this Russian nationalist who lauded Leonid Brezhnev's legacy was a "democrat in the rough" who would establish a free-market democracy. His stewardship of Russia is most notable for his initiation of two Chechen wars and his order to fire artillery at his own democratically elected Parliament. The United States anti-Gorbachev bias was expressed dramatically during Clinton's April 20–21 visit to Moscow when he met with Russian opposition leaders. Gennady Zyuganov, the Communist who was leading President Yeltsin in the polls, was among those invited to the meeting, and, according to the *New York Times*, "delivered a lengthy soliloquy" supporting "political pluralism, a mixed economy and freedom of speech." Mikhail Gorbachev, the former President who established Russian democracy against Zyuganov's fierce resistance and won the Nobel Peace Prize for ending the Cold War, was snubbed because, according to a senior United States official, "it would have upset Yeltsin far more to have him there than for Clinton to be talking to Zyuganov."

This may explain why Gorbachev is a Nobel Prize winner, whereas Clinton can't leave behind the nickname "Slick Willie."

CHAPTER VIII

BLACK DESTINY

Black political power is arguably sufficient to change the political landscape of the United States. The official results of the 2004 presidential election showed the Black vote delivering an *11.5 million* vote advantage to the Democratic ticket, based on a 90 percent Black solidarity. In 2008, if the Black turnout increases from the 13 percent of the total electorate recorded in 2004 to 14 percent, Blacks could potentially deliver a *15 million* vote advantage to the Democratic ticket.[1]

Given the decisive Black political power these statistics represent, coupled with steadfast Black loyalty to the Party over the past seven decades, the economic gains and political influence that Blacks have achieved over the past forty years, including the status of Black leaders within the Democratic Party, are pitifully small. This unacceptable situation is due primarily to a failure of Black leadership—a failure so fundamental and widespread that a wholesale leadership renewal should be considered.

Mired in nostalgia for the civil rights struggles and lacking a plan for the future, this ill-defined group has consistently advanced the interests of the Black middle class against the interests of the Black working class and poor and has opportunistically accommodated to the political status quo. Its exclusionary attitude toward the rising younger generation of leaders has been reflected in a patriarchal membership and an avoidance of meaningful debate.

In this context, achievements such as appointments to the highest government positions (including Secretary of State, United States Supreme Court Justice, Secretary of Defense, Chairman of the Joint Chiefs of Staff), and increased membership in the political leadership or corporate boardrooms are significant but of secondary importance. Individual successes are no longer of much practical value in themselves.

Symbolic acts associated with the past, such as the United States Senate apology for blocking anti-lynching legislation, are minor gestures. The only milestones that really matter are those marking tangible advancements in the condition of African-Americans as an entire people. Given the power we now command, the bulk of our political energy should be expended in pursuing these greater goals.

The vast majority of Blacks are concerned primarily with issues and results, rather than with style, personalities, process, rhetoric, and platforms. We judge political parties and candidates primarily by what they *do*, not by what they *say*. Varied individual and collective life experiences have taught most of us that only *progressive* candidates, whether white or Black, are willing to support the most vital collective Black interests. For me, these overriding interests are encapsulated in the following four demands:

1. Equal economic opportunity and equal treatment for all United States citizens, ultimately enforced by the federal government under the equal-treatment clause of the Fourteenth Amendment to the United States Constitution.

2. The formal acknowledgment, in the form of an amendment to the Preamble of the United States Constitution, which states that one of the purposes of our envisioned "more perfect Union" is to secure universal human rights as the undeni-

able birthright of every human being on the sovereign territory of the United States, and that our nation honors that birthright with regard to every human being on earth.

3. Acceptance of the principle that the promotion of the "general welfare" mandated by the Preamble to the United States Constitution is best served by guidelines based on President Abraham Lincoln's Gettysburg Address, President Franklin D. Roosevelt's Four Freedoms, and President John F. Kennedy's Inaugural Address.

4. Implementation of these general guidelines through an update of President Franklin Roosevelt's New Deal policies and practices.[2]

The official political spectrum has been condensed into three categories: *conservatives*, *liberals*, and *independents* (centrists). *Ultra-conservatives* (neoconservatives) hide unofficially among the conservatives, and *progressives* hide unofficially among the liberals. The real right and left (neofascists and neocommunists) have been officially eliminated from the political spectrum and driven underground. This terminology is used below to describe current Black political preferences.

1. Most liberals and progressives are Democrats or independents, whereas most conservatives and ultraconservatives are Republicans.

2. Conservatives and ultraconservatives almost always favor corporations and the wealthy over family businesses and the nonwealthy. Liberals genuinely try to favor everybody equally, but since this is rarely possible in practice, they usually end up favoring the wealthy. Progressives always favor the nonwealthy.

3. Ultraconservatives and conservatives tend to be racist; progressives and liberals tend to be antiracist. These perma-

nently "built-in" definitions stem from historical conflicts between the slave owners and the abolitionists, as well as from the experiences of slavery, the Civil War, and Reconstruction.

4. In a crunch, liberals usually appease conservatives on the issue of race. Only progressives are often willing to oppose racism without appeasing conservatives and sometimes even to attack ultra-conservatives openly as racists.

5. Progressives are reliable, permanent allies, with whom most Blacks share core interests. Neither liberals nor conservatives are our allies. Ultraconservatives are our permanent political enemies, and since most of us perceive today's Republican Party to be mainly an ultraconservative party, a significant number of us tend to treat all Republicans as our political enemies.

6. Organized labor has proved to be our most reliable ally outside of the political system. Since a large majority of Blacks are working-class and poor, our majority economic interests coincide with those of the organized labor movement. This is why we consistently support and join unions, including those that are racist to the point of segregating us into separate locals. Moreover, we are aware that when our political power increases, so does labor's, and vice versa.[3]

These perceptions and commitments explain why the Black vote has delivered, on the average, an 8 percent advantage to the Democratic ticket in the last eight presidential elections, contrasted with the 10.4 percent advantage delivered to the Republican ticket by the white vote.

Since 1944, no Democratic ticket, including the Truman and Kennedy tickets, has received a majority of the white vote.

This different political behavior reflects a Black-white difference in *cultural values*, not only a difference in political allegiance. A majority of Blacks tend to be guided by com-monly held *ethical commitments* derived from shared histor-ical experiences as an ethnic group, rather than by rigid moral commandments derived from absolute "good" and "evil."[4]

■ ■ ■

The United States popular culture attempts to control African-American collective memory by shaping the presen-tation of African-American history and the images of the leading African-American historical figures. Selected ideas from this distorted past then serve to constrict the present potential for the purpose of bolstering the official ideologi-cal status quo. Two examples of this kind come to mind.

Rev. Martin Luther King's historic address to the 1963 March on Washington in support of civil rights legislation has been officially enshrined in the trivialized form of a short excerpt restricted to his vision of an ideal future ("I had a dream"), while suppressing his searing indictment of the "nightmare" of poverty engulfing ghetto Blacks. Moreover, all references to his 1967–1968 public opposition to the Vietnam War, his linkage of class issues with civil rights issues, and calls for a radical restructuring of the political system are consistently ignored by both the liberal establishment and most of the civil rights leadership.

The historical record reveals that in 1964–1965, the younger, more radical wing of the civil rights movement split off from King and his progressive coalition to pursue the goal of "Black Power," meaning an equitable Black share of national political and economic power. For them, equal rights were not enough. Equal opportunity would have to accompany those rights, and independent political power was necessary to enforce equal opportunity.

The Black Power movement was generated by both the discontent of the Black working class, whose interests had been largely bypassed by the civil rights movement, and the gathering rebellion of the suffering ghetto masses whom liberal academics referred to as the "Black poor." Later their official classification would become the "Black underclass," a term that by 1969 included *one-half* of the entire Back population of our nation.[5]

The civil rights laws adopted in 1965 did little or nothing to break down the institutionalized racist barriers to equal opportunity, thus crippling the effectiveness of the highly touted Office of Equal Opportunity. The misnamed War on Poverty provided significant education and training to the ghetto poor but failed to guarantee either jobs or equal employment opportunity. The unintended net result was a continuing rise in poverty, compounded by an exponentially rising anger caused by the frustration of those who became educated and trained but met an absence of jobs.

The assassinations of President John F. Kennedy in 1963 and of Malcom X in 1965 both frightened and infuriated the ghetto poor. Kennedy had become a positive symbol for them because of his support for civil rights and his decisive use of regular army troops to suppress white mob violence in Mississippi. His eloquent acknowledgment of the poor and their plight in his Inaugural Address—"If a free society cannot help the many who are poor, it cannot save the few who are rich"—rang true to them. His violent death angered them profoundly, for they believed, probably correctly, that those who had killed him were those who sought to destroy them.

Malcolm's assassination in 1965 was taken as a direct personal assault. To them he was "a shining Black prince," and they identified with him. Soon after Malcolm's assassination, the late Ossie Davis replied to a magazine editor's question: "Why did you eulogize Malcolm X?" with the following "bottom line":

> I never doubted that Malcolm X . . . was always that rarest thing in the world among us Negroes: a true man.
>
> And if, to protect my relations with the many good white folks who make it possible for me to earn a fairly good living . . . I was too chicken, too cautious, to admit that fact when he was alive, I thought that at least now, when all the white folks are safe from him at last, I could be honest with myself enough to lift my hat for one final salute to that brave, ironic gallantry which was his style and hallmark, that shocking *zing* of fire-and-be-damned-to-you, so absolutely absent in every other Negro man I know, which brought him, too soon, to his death.

In 1999, thirty-four years after Malcom's assassination, his eldest daughter, Attallah Shabazz, wrote of him:

> Some have said that my father was ahead of his time, but the truth is he was on time and perhaps we were late. I trust that through his words we may come to respect all members of the human family as he did.[6]

Malcolm's Autobiography contains some of his most insightful comments. For example, he writes, "I've had enough of someone else's propaganda. . . . I'm a human being first and foremost, and as such I'm for whoever and whatever benefits humanity as a whole." Such a priority places *human* self-identification above *racial* self-identification and thus places Black-white relations on common *human* ground.

This comment marks Malcolm's transformation from a Black nationalist to a Black humanist after his pilgrimage to Mecca, a spiritual journey that caused him to break irrevocably with the sectarian nationalism of the Nation of Islam. It also points to one of the fundamental flaws in contemporary Black-nationalist ideology: its substitution of the *priority of narrow sectarian values* for the *priority of universal human values.*

Malcolm's exponential spiritual and intellectual growth stirred the imagination of Black Americans to an extent unmatched since Paul Robeson's two decades as "the King of Harlem" (1927–1932), "our Paul" (1933–1939), and "the tallest tree in our forest" (1940–1949). During Malcolm's time, even King could not equal his ability to capture the hearts of the Black poor. Only several years after Malcolm's assassination, when King led the Poor People's March, opposed the Vietnam War, and went to Memphis, where he supported the sanitation workers' strike and delivered his memorable "I Have Seen the Promised Land" sermon, did King enter the hearts of the Black poor to a degree unparalleled in the history of Black Americans.

Speaking metaphorically, if Robeson was "the tallest tree in our forest" and Malcolm was "our shining Black prince," then King was our Moses.

It was a great tribute to President John F. Kennedy when the hope he had given to the Black poor caused them to keep the peace in the ghettos after *their* president—the first one since Lincoln to acknowledge them and their history explicitly—had been assassinated. They paid an even greater tribute to Malcolm when, after his assassination, they rejected the second of his two proposed options, "the ballot or the bullet," and once more kept the peace.

However, the much maligned Black ghetto masses, contemptuously ridiculed by many middle-class Blacks, demonized by mainstream culture as the "underclass" and the "Black poor," and encompassing, according to official United States government estimates, *one-half of the black urban population*, paid the greatest tribute of all to Rev. King.

In 1968, when King was cut down as he walked in the footsteps of the legendary prophets of the past, they rose, but only momentarily, in rebellious fury. The arson and looting was only on a token scale compared to the previous sustained uprisings, and it ended as suddenly as it had begun.

It appears to me that the ghetto population was sending to its oppressors a message that might be paraphrased loosely as follows:

> We know who you are, and we recognize your awesome power. Our Moses and his predecessors have not been able to lead us to the Promised Land, but they have given to us the ability to distinguish friend from foe, and enough courage to resist by our own choice, rather than in response to provocation. The "fire next time," presaged by James Baldwin, will come if and when we decide to bring it on.

This renewed self-consciousness of the ghetto masses had been sparked by the successive waves produced by the civil rights struggles, the Black power movement, the antiwar movement, the Poor People's March, and the exponential growth of cultural nationalism. The result has been a dramatic rise in the degree of self-identification of the Black masses as the heirs, guardians, and disseminators of the cultural traditions of Southern field slaves. The continuing rise and proliferation of the rap and hip-hop subcultures as well as the developing use of DNA tests to trace slave ancestry bear witness to an irresistible Black determination to reclaim, preserve, and extend the collective Black historical memory.

■ ■ ■

Collective memory is the most powerful historical weapon available to any oppressed people. Its most effective use requires a three-step process: (1) the accurate perception of the present in the context of present beliefs (where are we?); (2) the accurate perception of the past in the context of past beliefs (where were we?); (3) the comparison of "where we were" with "where we are" in order to decide where to go and how to get there.

This is the process that has been initiated and sustained by the unsung struggles of Black masses over the past four decades. It is by the strength of their sturdy backs and unquenchable spirits that the wheel of African-American progress has been painfully rolled forward. Their incalculable sacrifice has been to bear the crushing burden of the drug wars, the mushrooming and poisonous prison system, the still-surging AIDS epidemic, and the collapsing public-education system that have ravaged the ghettos for decades without letup.

For the ghetto masses, "the fire this time" came and went during the 1960s and 1970s. Now is the time for them to call forth the legacies of the six most important Black historical "icons"—Nat Turner, Frederick Douglass, Dr. W. E. B. DuBois, Paul Robeson, Malcolm X, and Rev. Martin Luther King, Jr. These combined legacies have enabled the vast mass of Black Americans, from whom all of our talent and achievement arise in the first place, to acquire a collective wisdom sufficient to defeat a twenty-nine-year "colonization" drive.

President Kennedy's assassination on November 22, 1963, cut short his determined quest for equal rights and equal opportunity. From that moment until President Clinton's first Inauguration in January of 1993, United States government policy toward the Black ghetto masses consisted of a sophisticated adaptation of techniques perfected by the British colonial system, the South African apartheid system, and the slave system of the United States South. The stated objective of this policy was the elimination of the Black poor as a class.

A certified liberal, Democrat Daniel Moynihan, the late United States senator from New York, launched the campaign to colonize the ghetto with a report to President Lyndon Johnson titled *The Negro Family* (the "Moynihan Report").[7] In it, Moynihan provided the ideological and organizational foundation for a ghetto pacification program administered by the white-run Office of Equal Opportunity.

A lavishly funded colonial-style patronage infrastructure was deliberately substituted for the direct economic self-empowerment program, funded through large federal block grants and administered by accountable community leaders, which was demanded by Rev. King and his progressive supporters. As a result, the "War on Poverty" did little to aid the ghetto poor or to empower them to help themselves.

Instead it created a virtual "new class" of Black politicians, entrepreneurs, administrators, and other types of professionals to service and represent the ghetto population. This group resembled in some ways the indigenous administrations in the former British colonies. In any case, it was ultimately controlled by the predominantly white government personnel.

Moynihan's main practical recommendation profoundly affected the ghetto poor: end the draft and attract massive numbers of otherwise unemployed young Black males into an all-volunteer military. His reasoning was coldly logical: "If Negroes [would have been] represented in the same proportions in the military as they are in the population, ... the Negro male unemployment rate would have been 7.0 percent in 1964 instead of 9.1 percent."

In 1963 the Civil Rights Commission commented on the occupational aspect of military service for Negroes. "Negro enlisted men enjoy relatively better opportunities in the Armed Forces than in the civilian economy in every clerical, technical, and skilled field for which the data permit comparison. There is, however, an even more important issue involved in military service for Negroes. Service in the United States Armed Forces is the *only* [emphasis in original] experience open to the Negro American in which he is truly treated as an equal."

Moynihan pointed out that an end to the draft and the establishment of an all-volunteer Army would make it possible to attract a significant number of unemployable Black ghetto males into the armed forces. Confirming President Johnson's implementation of Moynihan's suggestion, Robert F. Kennedy commented during the 1968 presidential campaign that "If you look at any regiment or division of paratroopers in Vietnam, 45 percent of them are Black." This imbalance continues. At the beginning of the Iraq War in the spring of 2003, the overall presence of Blacks in the United

States armed forces had grown to over 20 percent, although only 9 percent of the total United States population is Black.

In a January 3, 1969 memorandum to newly elected President Richard Nixon, Moynihan wrote:

> Your task, then, is clear: to restore the authority of American institutions. Not, certainly, under that name, but with a clear sense that what is at issue is the continued acceptance by the great mass of people of the legitimacy and efficacy of the present arrangements of American society, and of our processes for changing those arrangements.
>
> The problem is not that one group in the population is beginning to react to centuries of barbarism by another group. The problem is that this cultural reaction among black [sic] militants is accompanied by the existence of a large, disorganized urban lower class which, like such groups everywhere, is unstable and essentially violent.
>
> The Negro lower class must be dissolved. This is the work of a generation, but it is time it began to be understood as a clear national goal. By lower class I mean the low income, marginally employed, poorly educated, disorganized slum dwellers who have piled up in our central cities over the past quarter century. I would estimate that they make up almost one half the total Negro population.
>
> It is this group that black [sic] extremists use to threaten white society with the prospect of mass arson and pillage. It is also this group that terrorizes and plunders the stable elements in the Negro community. . . . Take the urban lower class out of the pic-

ture and the Negro cultural revolution becomes an exciting and constructive development.

The Johnson Administration's implementation of the Moynihan Report evoked the sustained resistance of the ghetto masses. The attempt at domestic colonization was met by the domestic equivalent of a colonial liberation movement with a similarly high level of consciousness.

The August 3, 1968, edition of the *Chicago Daily Defender* published its first article in a series on the topic, "Is Genocide Possible in America?" Charles V. Hamilton, a Black political science professor at Roosevelt University wrote:

> The clear answer to this question must be "yes" . . . The American Indians know this. Japanese-Americans are well aware of this.

On September 7, 1968, the *Washington Afro-American* published an interview with Dr. Philip M. Hauser, Director of the Population Reference Bureau. According to Dr. Hauser,

> If we are not prepared to make the investment in human resources that is required, we will be forced to increase our investment in the Police, National Guard, and the Army. And possibly—it can happen here—we may be forced to resort to concentration camps and even genocide.[8]

When Dr. Hauser wrote his warning in 1968, the ghetto masses already knew whereof he spoke. They chose to endure, to wait until their time came and they were not alone. The eight-year respite (1992–1999) they experienced during the Clinton years was put to good use. By 2000, Black Americans had achieved a political solidarity that could deliver over 90 percent of the total Black vote to a preferred presidential candidate. Moreover, the turnout of registered Black voters had increased from 10 percent of the total turnout in 1992 to 13 percent in 2004.

In 2008, this figure is certain to be at least 14 percent. Therefore, if the approximately 90 percent Black voter solidarity achieved in 2000 and 2004 is maintained through 2008, Black Americans can deliver an advantage of 15 million popular votes to the 2008 Democratic presidential ticket. This means that the Black vote has become the decisive factor in any election in which the white vote is closely divided.

Moreover, despite massive Republican propaganda, bribes, and infiltration, Black voting solidarity has been increasing consistently—from 83 and 84 percent for Clinton in 1992 and 1996 to 92 percent and 91 percent in 2000 and 2004 for Gore and Kerry. With an outstanding Black personality, such as Barack Obama or Colin Powell, on the Democratic ticket as the 2008 vice presidential candidate, together with a young Southern economic populist like John Edwards heading the ticket, the Black turnout could be as high as 15 *percent* of the total electorate with a *96 percent* solidarity.

Such an optimal scenario could provide the Democratic ticket with an insuperable 22.7 million vote advantage in popular votes.

■ ■ ■

Quality of leadership is difficult to describe but easy to measure. It is measured, above all, by results. To the ghetto masses, leaders are those who *both* "talk the talk" *and* "walk the walk." The current Black civil rights leadership has lost every vestige of credibility in the eyes of the vast majority of Black Americans because for forty years it has done neither.

It appears to me that the same can be said of the national leadership of the Democratic Party and of the AFL-CIO. The recent split of the AFL-CIO, which has essentially divided the labor movement into its two original AFL and CIO components, has initiated an irrevocable process ending in the disintegration of the present political status quo. This traditional arrangement, which is based on an exclusive liberal/conservative two-party system, is collapsing before our eyes under the irresistible pressures of the digital information age, the ever-increasing corruption spread by corporate power, and the rapidly expanding gap between the wealthy and nonwealthy.

The present Republican administration has thoroughly corrupted the executive and legislative branches of government and is hell-bent on corrupting the judicial branch as well. It continues to trample the United States Constitution with such impunity that it has lost the support of a majority of the American people. Its credibility abroad is at an all-time low, and the current occupant of the White House is one of the least respected and most incompetent presidents in the history of our nation.

He is also the instrument through which the ultraconservative wing of the Republican Party has won control of the entire federal government and the governments of many key states. The ultraconservatives are driven by religious and ideological fanaticism. Their rhetoric and their behavior demonstrate that they respect no rules except their own, violate the United States Constitution at will, and seek to institutionalize their power by any means necessary.

The Democratic Party, paralyzed by the political cow-ardice of its liberal wing, has shunned the role of a real oppo-sition party because that would require it to appeal directly to all the people with a substantive program that promotes the general welfare rather than corporate welfare. It would mean empowering the entire electorate, including the 42 percent of eligible voters who in the past have chosen not to vote because their interests are ignored.

This vast mass of eligible nonvoters is mostly working class and poor, with annual incomes under $50,000, and a high proportion of Blacks and Latinos. Half of them, or 21 percent of all eligible voters, have annual incomes below $30,000. About one-fifth of them, or 8 percent of all eligible voters, have annual incomes below $15,000. This enormous potential political army is not ideological, nor is it primarily concerned with "moral values."

Its primary concern is with economic issues and results. It is also concerned with war and peace, since its youth are pri-marily the ones who enlist in the all-volunteer armed forces because economic and educational opportunities are far greater there than in civilian life.

These eligible nonvoters are the real swing vote, rather than the current middle-class (annual income over $75,000), pre-dominantly white 5 percent of eligible voters who currently hold the balance of power between liberals and conservatives in the two-party system.

In this context, it appears to me that the only way to encourage most nonvoters to vote is to break up the two-party system. The best way to achieve this would be to cre-ate a Progressive Party based on issues and results, which counterposes a pro-people's platform to the conservative pro-corporate platform.

Since this Progressive Party would be based on issues rather than on ideology, it would be a genuine left on issues but would not be identified with traditional left-wing ideology. By contrast, the Republican Party, which is based on ideology rather than on issues, would be identified as a party of the right. The Democratic Party would then be identified as a center party. The ideologically-based left groups and the neofascists on the right would continue to be excluded by all three major parties as a matter of their official policy.

In this political environment, all eligible voters would have a clear choice; the issues would match up with the parties, and major-party candidates at all political levels would be forced to campaign as progressives, rightists, or centrists. Under these conditions, the results of elections would predictably correspond to the effects on people's lives. Consequently, the electorate could hold the political system directly accountable. This is what true political democracy is supposed to be.

Historical experience has shown that political upheavals of this kind occur only in conjunction with major mass movements, such as the mass organization of industrial workers in the 1930s, the civil rights movement of 1945–1948, and the civil rights movement of the 1960s. Of these three mass movements, only the popular upsurge of the 1940s in the wake of World War II produced a Progressive Party. It failed because the Democratic Party, under incumbent President Truman, coopted its entire populist domestic program.

The situation in America today is far different. The incumbent President has been exposed as a rightist; the nation is faced with simultaneous economic and foreign policy crises; the Iraq War is reminiscent of the Vietnam War; both major parties are in disarray, and the political system has failed in two successive national elections. *Consequently, I believe that*

*conditions are ripe for an issue-oriented mass movement lead-
ing to the creation of a Progressive Party.*

The political objective of this movement would be to ter-
minate the present liberal-conservative political monopoly by
creating a third party that offers the clear choice of a government of the people, by the people, for the people instead
of a government by, of, and for the special interests. The base
of the party would consist of Blacks, Latinos, the labor
unions that have split from the AFL-CIO, and white progressives. This would leave the two major parties with liberals
and conservatives *only*.

The Progressive Party would focus mainly on attracting
the large nonvoting constituency of households with an
annual income below $50,000. It would appeal to them by pri-
oritizing their *economic interests. Actual voters* in this category constituted 45 percent of the 2004 vote.

Households with an annual income between $50,000 and
$75,000 constituted 23 percent of the total 2004 vote and had
essentially the same overall economic interests and priorities as those having an annual income below $50,000.

Thus, collectively, these two categories constituted 45 percent + 23 percent = 68 percent of the total 2004 vote. If one-
third of the present nonvoting constituency consisting of 42
percent of the total elible vote were to be inspired to vote in
2008, about 72 percent of all eligible voters would cast ballots,
compared to 58 percent in 2004.

I estimate that about 75 percent of the voters in the 2008
presidential election will belong to households with an annual
income below $75,000. This majority constituency shares
common economic interests, similar social outlooks, and a
powerful need for spiritual sustenance. It appears to me that
a strong majority of this group of voters would prefer candidates running on a platform based on the following planks:

- An economic program that pursues economic fairness and the general welfare. The implementation of the program would be based on President Franklin D. Roosevelt's "New Deal" principles stemming from the first two of his Four Freedoms—freedom *from* fear and freedom *from* want.

- Uncompromising defense of all existing civil rights and their full enforcement by the federal government under a constitutional mandate. The guiding principles should be the last two of Roosevelt's Four Freedoms—freedom *of* speech and freedom *of* religion.

- Uncompromising support of *universal human rights.*

- Commitment to the universal *faith*, which is nondenominational, rather than to a *religion* which is denominational. Self-identification as a "Judeo-Christian," rather than as either a "Jew" or a "Christian."

- Unequivocal opposition to the Iraq War, coupled with an exit strategy based on the complete withdrawal of United States military forces by December 2006, one year after the December 2005 Iraqi general election.

Such a program would probably win the support of a solid majority of voters, provided that the main divisive issues in the 2008 election are economic, rather than "the war on terror," race, and "moral values." This can be achieved by approaching social, cultural and foreign-policy issues *exclusively* from a positive, unifying point of view rather than from a protest standpoint. Always shine some light instead of cursing the darkness.

This political environment would guarantee the increased participation and solidarity of the households having an annual income below $75,000. Since potentially they will represent 75 percent of the total vote in 2008, they will decide the election.

In 2004, this category, constituting 68 percent of the total vote, *voted against Bush* by a narrow *1.7 percent* even though John Kerry, the Democratic presidential candidate, virtually ignored their interests.[9]

Thus, it appears that the entire constituency with annual incomes below $75,000, or about two-thirds of all 2004 voters, had little enthusiasm for either candidate. Small wonder, since neither candidate addressed these citizens' core economic interests. They were both obsessed with courting the middle and upper classes almost exclusively. It is for this reason that the election turned on divisive issues other than economic ones.

It would appear self-evident that an appeal directly to the voting constituency with annual incomes below $75,000 would be highly successful. For example, the subgroup with annual incomes between $30,000 and $75,000 voted *against* the Democratic ticket by 53 percent to 47 percent in 2004, giving Bush a *3.2 million* vote advantage. However, if this subgroup had voted *for* the Democratic ticket by 55 percent to 45 percent because of a Democratic platform that had a powerful economic appeal, Kerry would have gained a *5.4 million* vote advantage and won the election.

It appears to me that if the Democratic Party were to focus *primarily* on attracting voters in households having an annual income below $75,000, the Democratic Party would almost certainly win a decisive victory in the general election of 2008.

The Democratic Party can win the 2008 election only if it

appeals to these voters with a program that unequivocally prioritizes their economic interests. For example, the Democratic platform would have to demand the repeal of the Bush tax cuts for all households having annual incomes above $100,000, reject the privatization of social security, support universal federally funded health care, support *fair* trade instead of *free* trade, and call for the regulation of large corporations.

At the same time, the winning platform would have to be restricted to potentially majority positions on race, social issues, and "moral values." For example:

■ [On race]: Guarantee the continuation of all civil rights legislation currently on the books, as well as the *federal enforcement* of all civil rights laws. Guarantee federal enforcement of *equal opportunity* as well as civil rights.

■ [On social issues]: Insist on the constitutional *right to privacy* under the First Amendment, and demand federal enforcement of the *equal-treatment* clause of the Fourteenth Amendment.

■ [On "moral values"]: Identify with *Judeo-Christian ethical values.*

Such a platform requires a strong presidential ticket.

■ ■ ■

Mass political parties can be built successfully only if, at the same time, there is a large uncommitted constituency and one of the major parties splits into two large factions, one of which is ready to leave the party. Even with these two prerequisites, a successful overall process must occur in stages that are synchronized with local and national elections.

At present, the Democratic Party is sharply divided between liberal and progressive factions. This is manifested by the tension between the progressive majority on the Democratic National Committee and the liberal Democratic Leadership Council; between liberal Senators Harry Reid, Joseph Biden, and Hillary Clinton and progressive Senators Barbara Boxer, Ted Kennedy, and Barack Obama; between the Black Caucus and the conservative Southern Democrats in the House of Representatives; and so on. It is also reflected in the recent AFL-CIO split in which the departing leadership supports progressive Democrats and the status-quo leadership supports liberals.

In these circumstances, the process of building the Progressive Party could consist of the following stages:

During the first stage, progressives inside the Democratic Party would conduct an uncompromising struggle to unite the Party behind a progressive platform and a ticket for the 2008 elections. That ticket could consist of John Edwards, a white Southern economic populist, for president, and Barack Obama, the outstanding Black senator from Illinois who consistently evokes Franklin D. Roosevelt's New Deal, for vice president. The platform would be based on a domestic fair economic deal reminiscent of President Franklin Roosevelt's New Deal and a multilateral foreign policy that rejects the Bush Doctrine of preemptive war.

The uncompromising campaign within the Democratic Party would have to aim at a solid progressive majority on the Democratic National Committee and the replacement of liberal chairman Howard Dean by a certifiable progressive.

Moreover, the progressive caucus of the party would be well-advised to declare its unwavering commitment to an Edwards-Obama ticket as early as possible. This tactic would exclude their support of any liberal presidential contenders such as the current front-runners (for example, Senators Hillary Clinton of New York and Joseph Biden of Delaware).

If this step is successfully completed by the time of the 2006 congressional elections, the Democratic Party will have effectively been transformed into a progressive party under another name. Consequently, no further steps would be required. If this result has not yet been achieved, then the second stage should be initiated.

The second stage should begin immediately after the 2006 primary vote. Those progressive Democrats who feel inclined to do so should be encouraged to leave the Democratic party and reregister as independents. The reregistration should be carried out after the casting of ballots in the November 2006 election. Then independent progressives should form a progressive third party. A founding convention should be held in July of 2007 to hammer out a platform, elect a national leadership, organize effective participation in the 2007 local elections, and select a preferred presidential ticket for the 2008 presidential elections.

The early selection of a preferred 2008 ticket is critical. It must be consistent with a progressive platform that takes unequivocal positions on the most controversial issues, yet reflects the political mood of the majority of the population. This means that a progressive program and a ticket that will certainly implement the program must appeal to a voting majority that wants a liberal-conservative compromise which appears to be more liberal than progressive. Consequently, the new Progressive Party must present itself as a unifying party of the majority, rather than as a party of the traditional left.

One way of solving this problem consists of the following. The platform should be general, rather than specific. Its theme should be something like "Out of today's two warring Americas, one—the America of Abraham Lincoln, Franklin D. Roosevelt, and John F. Kennedy." Controversial issues, including the controversial economic ones, should be framed in generalized terms, some of which have an encoded meaning:

■ Economic fairness with economic growth.

■ A multilateralist foreign policy.

■ Deficit reduction rather than tax breaks for the wealthy.

■ Peace with honor; not preemptive war.

■ Group identity with pluralism. [To Blacks and Latinos, this means "cultural diversity instead of cultural uniformity," or "the mosaic, not the melting pot." These phrases are far less acceptable to whites than the less controversial "group identity with pluralism" which has the same meaning if "group identity" is placed first.]

■ Fair trade, not free trade. [Code for "repeal NAFTA and CAFTA!"]

■ Equal opportunity with diversity.

■ The priority of people over property.

■ Affirmative action: mend it, don't end it.

- Defend the United States Constitution with its 26 Amendments; reject "original intent."[10]

- We are a Judeo-Christian nation, rather than an exclusively Christian nation.

Since the American people are unlikely to vote for an untried progressive president, the ticket should be led by a distinguished liberal with the recognized capacity to govern the nation well. The second slot should go to a Southern economic populist, preferably John Edwards.

Colin Powell, liberal Republican, former National Security Adviser to the President, the first Black Chairman of the Joint Chiefs of Staff, and the first Black Secretary of State, would be the ideal third-party presidential candidate. Moreover, he is by far the best conceivable candidate for the United States presidency. A patriot with decades of military service, including combat in the Vietnam War and overall command of the first Persian Gulf War, which was the most successful campaign in U.S. military history, he achieved the status of the world's most respected and effective negotiator and diplomat prior to being deliberately misled by CIA Director George Tenet.

Powell has made it clear publicly that he is politically independent despite his close association with many leading Republicans. He identifies himself emphatically as an African-American, and expresses his beliefs accordingly. In his autobiography he wrote:

> The Republican Convention [of 1992], with its racial overtones and troubling mix of politics and religion, had left a bad taste in the mouth of even middle-of-the-road Americans ....

The hard-won civil rights legislation of the 1960s, which I benefited from, was fought for by presently derided liberals, courageous leaders who won these gains over the opposition of those hiding behind transparent arguments of "states rights" and "property rights."

Equal rights and equal opportunity . . . mean just that. They do not mean preferential treatment.

I am . . . a champion of public secondary and higher education. I will speak out for them and support them for as long as I have the good sense to remember where I came from.

To sum up my political philosophy, I am a fiscal conservative with a social conscience. I have found my philosophy, if not my political affiliation. Neither of the two major parties fits me comfortably in its present state. . . .

I am troubled by the political passion of those on the extreme right who seem to claim divine wisdom on political as well as spiritual matters. God provides us with guidance and inspiration, not a legislative agenda. I am disturbed by the class and racial undertones beneath their rhetoric.

On the other side of the spectrum, I am put off by patronizing liberals who claim to know what is best for society but devote little thought to who will eventually pay the bills. I question the priorities of those liberals who lavish so much attention on individual license and entitlement that little concern is left for the good of the community at large.

I distrust rigid ideology from any direction, and I am discovering that many Americans feel just as I do. The time may be at hand for a third major party to emerge to represent this sensible center of the American political spectrum.[11]

Since Colin Powell explicitly rejects both George W. Bush's right-wing conservatism and Bill Clinton's neoliberal "third way," it would appear that the "sensible center" he represents is a cross between an updated New-Deal progressivism and Jimmy Carter's fiscally conservative liberalism. This position coincides with that of a majority of white voters. Consequently, I believe that a Powell-Edwards third-party ticket would win a landslide victory in 2008. However, the new Progressive Party would have to settle for a liberal president rather than a progressive one.

■　■　■

The sustained cultural awareness and self-identification of the Black ghetto masses, combined with their continuing oppression, explain the rapidly growing power of the Black vote. The struggles of these millions over the past thirty-seven years since King helped them to complete the self-emancipation of their minds from bondage, and have given them experience in exercising their free wills collectively. Now they require only a collective leadership which they themselves will choose.

Their prophets have come, empowered them, and departed. Now they, like their counterparts in every corner of Mother Earth, hold their destiny in their own hands. As a consequence, ghetto Blacks have become the critical swing vote in U.S. politics, and only they will decide how and when they will swing.

The mass media have been so obsessed with the success story of the Black middle class that over half of the Black population has remained all but invisible to the general public. Now, to the chagrin of the white political establishment, their Black surrogates are politically helpless. And the Black politicians who pretend that their endorsements make a significant difference in how the Black vote will be distributed are, without exception, either deluded or trying to fool the white establishment.

The mass media are feverishly attempting to neutralize, divert, dilute, and otherwise weaken or corrupt the cultural coherence and spiritual power of the Black ghetto culture. Billions of dollars are being spent for the purpose of buying out or otherwise controlling Black media and other instruments of cultural communication. Similar efforts have been underway throughout the educational system to achieve the cultural assimilation of ghetto youth into the mainstream culture.

However, all of these attempts have met with dismal failure because of the incompatibility of the values espoused by the popular culture with the core values of Black culture.

The highly commercialized mainstream culture worships materialism, placing the acquisition of property above all else. While providing a spectacularly varied external life, it does little to nurture the growth of a deep inner life. An obsession with superficial and narrowly defined physical beauty is aggressively cultivated, while the appreciation of spiritual beauty is discouraged.

Performance is valued above artistry in our popular culture. The mastery of *information* and power over the external world are placed ahead of the mastery of *knowledge* and *harmony* with the environment. The popular culture pressures people to think as one while acting individually for personal benefit, whereas a healthy society teaches people to think independently while acting collectively for the common good.

As the world enters the digital age, the cultures of the East and of Eurasia are advancing at a far more rapid rate than Western cultures. In the West, besieged by fear of terrorism and wracked with anxiety over a declining capacity to dominate world affairs, many Americans of faith are turning to the Bible for comfort and reassurance. They seek to reinforce their faith. In times like these, would-be leaders must speak to this rapidly growing constituency.

Inevitably, the political landscape becomes cluttered with all manner of demagogues, mountebanks, and outright political gangsters who seek to exploit the popular yearning. However, true prophets also appear, and somehow the great majority of the people always manage to discern them. They are quiet truth tellers, speaking sparingly and teaching only when asked or when a situation commands it. Traveling with no identification, without cross or crown, until their time comes, they arrive on time and leave on time.

■ ■ ■

Today's task is to complete the unfinished American revolution by fulfilling the combined promises of Lincoln's "New birth of freedom"; Roosevelt's "Freedom from fear, Freedom from want, Freedom of speech, Freedom of religion"; and Kennedy's call to "struggle against the common enemies of man—tyranny, poverty, disease, and war itself." This goal can be reached only if the present bankrupt governmental infrastructure is rebuilt anew on the basis of the behest in the Preamble of the United States Constitution to "promote the general welfare."

George W. Bush, an utterly incompetent president, is the personal symbol of the failed administration he heads. The arguably preventable disaster of 9/11, the certainly avoidable disaster of New Orleans, and the chosen calamity of the Iraq War are the results of this failure. The unnecessary human suffering in New Orleans and along the Gulf Coast in the wake of Hurricane Katrina is due to the deliberate and cruel neglect of the Black and poor by an irredeemably racist institutional infrastructure.

Consequently, the entire United States top executive leadership, including Vice President Richard Cheney and President George W. Bush, should be removed by forced resignation or impeachment on the ground of criminal negligence. The American people must accept the responsibility for carrying out such a judgment.

It was through Rev. King that the meek freed themselves from psychological bondage to seek their own destiny on the strength of their own free will.

The time has come when the meek shall inherit the earth. Most of us Blacks identify with the "meek" everywhere, and we, like the rest of the meek, feel and know that it is time for all of us to join together to inherit the earth through the power of our numbers, our unity, and our shared faith. The power to perceive, the courage to resist, and our own free will are enough to make this come about.

Paraphrasing Galatians,

Henceforth, let none trouble us, for we bear in our bodies the marks of Jesus.

NOTES

1. Had the Black vote split evenly between the Democratic and Republican Parties in the 2004 presidential election, a landslide Republican victory by *14.5 million* votes would have resulted. The official advantage awarded to the Republican ticket from the white vote was *15.7 million* votes. The official combined Black, Hispanic, and Asian vote gave the Democratic ticket a *12.7 million* vote advantage. The official net result was a *3.0 million* vote "win" for the Republican ticket (15.7—12.7 = 3.0).

   If all Black registered voters had been allowed to vote without illegal interference and the vote count had not been fraudulent, the Black vote would have delivered a *12.3 million* vote advantage to the Democrats, along with a *4 million* vote advantage from the combined Hispanic and Asian vote. The Republican advantage from the white vote would have been *12.9 million* votes, and the net result would have been a *3.4 million* vote victory for the Democratic ticket.

2. Philip A. Klinkner with Rogers M. Smith, *The Unsteady March*, Chicago, University of Chicago Press, 1999; James M. McPherson, *Abraham Lincoln and the Second American Revolution*, New York, Oxford University Press, 1991; Benjamin Quarles, *Lincoln and the Negro*, New York, Da Capo Press, 1990.

3. Ibid.

4. Black culture sees the Universe as a natural whole with positive and negative attributes, and Black philosophy teaches us to be in harmony with Nature—to *experience* life, rather than to seek the *meaning* of life.

5. See the seminal "The Negro Lower Class," a January 3, 1969, confidential memorandum written by Daniel Moynihan to President-elect Richard Nixon. (Persons inside the Nixon administration leaked parts of this secret memo to the press.)

6. Malcolm X with the assistance of Alex Haley, *The Autobiography of Malcolm X*, New York, Ballantine Books (hardcover edition), 1999. The "shining Black prince" quote is from Ossie Davis's eulogy of Malcolm X.

7. Office of Policy Planning and Research, Washington, D.C., United States Department of Labor, March, 1965.

8. Samuel F. Yette, *The Choice*, P.O. Box 2071, Silver Spring, Maryland, Cottage Books, (re: genocide); Harrison E. Livingstone, *Killing Kennedy*, New York, Carroll & Graf Publishers, Inc., 1995; James DiEugenio and Lisa Pease eds., *The Assassinations*, P.O. Box 13067, Los Angeles, CA 90013, Feral House, 2003; William F. Pepper, *Orders to Kill*, New York, Warner Books, 1995.

9. An important voter subgroup within this broader category—households with an annual income between $50,000 and $75,000 which accounted for

23 percent of the total vote—*voted against Kerry* by a large margin: *56 percent* to *43 percent.*This vote contrasts dramatically with the vote of the subgroup consisting of the poorest households with annual incomes below $30,000. These voters, who represented *23 percent* of the total vote (about the same percentage as the $50,000-$75,000 subgroup) voted *against Bush* by a whopping 60 percent to 40 percent because he had made them suffer economically. The subgroup with annual household incomes between $30,000 and $50,000 split almost evenly, *50 percent against Kerry and 49 percent against Bush.*

10. The original intent of the delegates who adopted the United States Constitution was to create a state that was half union and half confederacy, while stipulating the goal of "a more perfect union" in the Preamble without a time frame. Accepting the principle of "original intent" would mean that the United States Supreme would have license to interpret the *present* United States Constitution in accordance with the Court majority's speculation about what the Founding Fathers had in mind more than two centuries ago. Obviously, this is a bad idea.

11. *My American Journey*, Colin Powell, with Joseph E. Persico, Random House, N.Y., 1995.

THE ANATOMY OF TWO VOTE FRAUDS

I. THE 2000 ELECTIONS

THE ESTIMATED COUNT WAS:

Total vote 111.0 million; Gore 52.7 million; Bush 49.9 million; Nader 4.1 million; Invalid 4.3 million. Gore wins by 2.8 million votes (2.6 percent).

THE OFFICIAL COUNT WAS:

Total vote 111.0 million; Gore 51.0 million; Bush 50.5 million; Nader 3.9 million; Invalid 5.6 million. Gore wins by 0.5 million votes (0.5 percent).

THE *NET* ESTIMATED AMOUNT OF FRAUD WAS:

1.7 million (reduction of Gore vote) + 0.6 million (increase of Bush vote) + 0.2 million ("disappearance" of 0.2 million Nader votes) + 1.3 million (increase of Invalid votes) = 3.8 million.

Note: The exit polls and vote counts in their original format presented Valid votes only, while ignoring Invalid votes. All widely published analyses of and reports on the election returns were based on disputable figures for Valid votes, rather than on indisputable figures for Total votes. My analysis is based entirely on the indisputable figures for the

Overall Total votes—i.e., vote totals that include all Invalid votes. As a result, my analysis is easily verified, since the total number of Valid votes plus the the total number of Invalid votes must always add up to a fixed and verified Overall Total number. All percentages are given relative to the Overall Total, rather than the Valid Total. Thus, any fraud is revealed through its simultaneous alteration of both the Valid vote and the Invalid vote. Moreover, any fraudulent switch of votes from one category to another must be compensated by switching an equal number of different votes.

THE FRAUD WAS PERPETRATED AS FOLLOWS:

A. 1.4 million *Valid White* votes cast for Gore were invalidated, reducing his vote from 52.7 million to 51.3 million, and increasing the Invalid vote from 4.3 million to 5.7 million. [This fraud amounted to 1.4 million votes.]

B. The 1.4 million Gore votes that had been invalidated had to be accounted for, since they had been officially counted as Valid. Consequently, their invalidation had to be covered up with 1.4 million other votes. Most of these (1.1 million) were found by reducing the original *Total Black* vote by 1.1 million from 12.9 million to 11.8 million (from 11 percent to 10 percent of the Total vote) and declaring that the exit polls for the Black vote were wrong. Since the *Total Valid* vote had to remain the same, and the Invalid votes had already been altered by 1.4 million, the original *Total White* vote was raised by 1.1 million from 88.8 million to 89.9 million (from 77 percent to 78 percent of the Total vote). [This fraud amounted to 1.1 x 2 = 2.2 million votes.]

C. The *White Invalid* vote had been increased by 1.4 million formerly *Valid White* votes, and therefore 1.4 million other *White Invalid* votes had to be accounted for. Of these, 0.6 million were accounted for by switching 0.6 million *Black Invalid* votes into the *White Invalid* category, increasing the *White Invalid* votes from 4.6 million to 5.2 million. The *Hispanic Invalid* vote was decreased by 0.3 million from 0.3 million to zero, and these 0.3 million Invalid votes were switched to the *White Invalid* category, raising it from 5.2 million to the official 5.5 million. These manipulations accounted for 0.6 + 0.3 = 0.9 million out of the 1.4 million original *Valid White Gore* votes that had been invalidated, leaving 0.5 million to be covered up. [This fraud amounted to 0.9 million votes.]

D. The 4.1 million Nader vote was reduced by 0.2 million to 3.9 million by "losing" 0.2 million Nader votes and assigning them to Bush, increasing his total from 49.9 million to 50.1 million. [This fraud amounted to 2 x 0.2 = 0.4 million.]

E. The 92 percent Gore–6 percent Bush–2 percent Nader split of the Black vote was altered to 90 percent Gore–8 percent Bush–0 percent Nader, switching 0.3 million *Black Gore* votes to Bush. This decreased Gore's vote from 51.3 million to 51.0 million and increased Bush's vote from 50.1 million to 50.4 million. Since 0.3 million *Black Nader* votes were switched to Bush and only 0.2 million Nader votes were "lost," 0.1 million Nader votes would remain unaccounted for. The *Total Black* vote was correspondingly reduced by 0.1 million from 12.3 million to 12.2 million. The 0.1 million discrepancy was covered by "losing" 0.1 million out of the "lost" 0.2 million *Invalid Nader* votes. This also reduced the total Invalid vote from 5.7 million to the official 5.6 million. At the same time, the 0.1 million plus Bush's added 0.3 million accounted for 0.4 million of the unaccounted-for 0.5 million identified in paragraph C above. Finally, the last 0.1 million of the "lost" *Invalid Nader* votes were switched to Bush, raising his total from 50.4 million to the official 50.5 million and covering the last 0.1 million unaccounted-for votes. [This fraud amounted to 2 x 0.3 + 0.1 + 0.1 = 0.8 million.]

F. Thus, the *total* fraud is significantly greater than the net fraud of 3.8 million votes: 1.4 + 2.2 + 0.4 + 0.8 = 4.8 million votes.

G. The switching operations are reflected in the Invalid category changes when the actual and official results are compared.

1. The number of *White Invalid* votes increased by 2.3 million from 3.2 million to 5.5 million.

2. The number of *Black Invalid* votes decreased by 0.7 million, from 0.7 million to zero.

3. The number of *Hispanic Invalid* votes decreased by 0.3 million, from 0.3 million to zero.

4. The total number of Invalid votes increased by 1.3 million, from 4.3 million to 5.6 million.

5. The total number of Invalid votes switched is +2.3 - 0.7 - 0.3 = +1.3 million which equals the increase of the total number of Invalid votes from 4.3 million to 5.6 million.

[Note: Tables illustrating this complex set of interconnected switching operations can be found in Appendix B below.]

II. THE 2004 ELECTIONS

THE ESTIMATED COUNT WAS:

Total vote 128.7 million; Bush 58.7 million; Kerry 62.1 million; Nader 1.3 million; Invalid votes 6.6 million; Kerry wins by 3.4 million votes (2.8 percent).

THE OFFICIAL COUNT WAS:

Total vote 128.7 million; Bush 62.0 million; Kerry 59.0 million; Nader 1.1 million; Invalid votes 6.6 million; Bush "wins" by 3.0 million votes (2.5 percent).

THE *NET* TOTAL AMOUNT OF FRAUD WAS:

3.1 million Kerry votes switched to Bush, plus 0.2 million Nader votes switched to Bush, for a total of $(3.1 \times 2) + (0.2 \times 2) = 6.6$ million.

THE FRAUD WAS PERPETRATED AS FOLLOWS:

A. 0.7 million *Valid White Kerry* votes were invalidated, reducing the Kerry total from 62.1 million to 61.4 million. The number of *White Invalid* votes was thereby increased from 4.3 million to 5.0 million, and the total number of Invalid votes was increased from 6.6 million to 7.3 million. The 0.1 million *Black Nader* votes were temporarily "lost" and kept in reserve for later manipulations. [This fraud amounted to 0.7 + 0.1 = 0.8 million votes.]

B. 0.95 million *Valid Black Kerry* and *Hispanic Kerry* votes were switched from Kerry to Bush, reducing Kerry's total from 61.4 million to 60.45 million, and increasing Bush's total from 58.7 million to 59.65 million. (The net Bush gain was 1.9 million.)

THIS SWITCHING OPERATION WAS ACCOMPLISHED AS FOLLOWS:

1. The estimated 91 percent Kerry–8 percent Bush–0.7 percent Nader split of the Black vote was altered to 88 percent Kerry–11 percent Bush–0 percent Nader. This switch of 3 percent of the total Black vote of 16.7 million from Kerry to Bush corresponded to a switch of 0.5 million Black votes from Kerry to Bush (a net Bush gain of 1.0 million votes). At the same time, the 0.7 percent of the Black vote (0.1 million votes) that was cast for Nader was made to "disappear."

2. The estimated Kerry–Bush split of the Hispanic vote was altered to Bush's advantage in at least nine states. This switch of about 0.45 million Hispanic votes from Kerry to Bush produced a net Bush gain of 0.9 million votes. [The fraud involved in steps 1 and 2 amounted to 1.0 + 0.9 + 0.1 = 2.0 million votes.]

C. The *White Kerry* vote was decreased by 1.95 million, reducing his total from 60.45 million to 58.5 million. The *White Bush* vote was increased by 2.85 million from 59.65 million to 62.5 million.

THE 1.95 + 2.85 = 4.8 MILLION WHITE VOTES REQUIRED FOR THIS PUR-
POSE WERE SOUGHT IN THE FOLLOWING MANNER:

1. 2.1 million potentially valid Hispanic votes which had been
cast by registered Hispanic voters were invalidated and reclassified as White votes. The official Hispanic vote was falsely
declared to be 6 percent of the total vote rather than the actual
8 percent. The actual 77 percent White vote was correspondingly
raised to a fictitious 79 percent.

These 2.1 million "White" votes remained in the Invalid category, and 2.1 million other *Invalid White* votes plus the 0.7 million
invalidated *Kerry White* votes (a total of 2.8 million) were available
for switching. The assignment of the 0.7 million votes restored the
total number of Invalid votes to the original 6.6 million.

Another 0.1 million votes available for switching consisted of
the 0.1 million *Black Nader* votes that had "disappeared" (see
Point 1 of Paragraph II above). This brought the total number of
available votes to 2.1 + 0.7 + 0.1 = 2.9 million, short of the
required 4.8 million by 1.9 million. [This fraud amounted to 2.1
+ 0.7 + 0.1 = 2.9 million votes.]

D. The 1.9 million additional *Invalid White* votes required for switching, plus the 2.1 million White votes required to account for the fake
White votes that formerly were the 2.1 million invalidated Hispanic
votes, added up to 4.0 million White votes.

1. The actual 42.6 percent Kerry—56.2 percent Bush split of the
White vote was altered to 41 percent Kerry–57.8 percent Bush. This
switch of 1.6 percent of the total White vote of 94.7 million from
Kerry to Bush corresponded to a switch of 1.5 million White votes
from Kerry to Bush. The net change of 3.0 million in the White
vote accounts for the 2.1 million invalidated Hispanic votes fraudulently reclassified as "White," plus 0.9 million of the additional
White votes required.

2. There remained 1.0 million White votes still to be accounted for. These were created by switching 1.0 million *Valid Hispanic* votes from Kerry to Bush, invalidating them, converting them into *Invalid White* votes, and then switching them to account for the remaining 1.0 million unaccounted for White votes. This was accomplished by altering the Kerry-Bush split of Hispanic votes from the estimated 68 percent Kerry–31percent Bush to 56 percent Kerry–43 percent Bush. This 12 percent wing of the total official Hispanic vote of 8.0 million equaled 0.96 million, or 1.0 million rounded off to the nearest 0.1 million. However, the problem of an extra 10 million Invalid votes was created, inflating the number of invalidated votes to 7.6 million from 6.6 million. This difficulty was solved by switching from Bush to Kerry 0.5 million *Invalid White* votes that were formerly Hispanic votes, and reclassifying the other 0.5 million newly invalidated *Bush White* votes as *Valid Hispanic* votes, thus making the other newly created *Invalid White* votes "disappear." At the same time, Bush's 4.0 million "near-blowout" of Kerry (62.5 million to 58.5 million) was reduced to a more reasonable 3.0 million vote "victory" (62.0 million to 59.0 million).[This fraud amounted to $(2 \times 1.5) + (2 \times 1.0)$ = 5.0 million votes.]

The total fraud amounted to $0.8 + 2.0 + 2.9 + 5.0 = 10.7$ million votes.

E. In order to perpetrate vote fraud on such an enormous scale, the Republican-controlled election machinery had to create an abnormally large pool of Invalid votes. It accomplished this goal by illegally manipulating massive numbers of Hispanic, White, and Black votes. In addition, at least one million registered Black voters were illegally disfranchised, mostly in states governed by Republicans.

F. The number of Invalid votes in 2004 was abnormally high compared to 2000 when there were actually 4.3 million Invalid votes out of 111.0 million total votes cast (3.9 percent). In 2004, there were actually 6.6 million Invalid votes out of 128.7 million total votes cast (5.1 percent).

This invalidation rate is inordinately high—1.3 times the rate in 2000. This in itself is highly suspicious. If the invalidation rate in 2004 had been the same as it was in 2000, there would have been 5.0 million Invalid votes, or 1.6 million less than the actual 6.6 million.

G. The changes within the Invalid category of votes reflect the fraud. For example, the number of *White Invalid* votes was altered by 0.7 million from 4.3 million to 5.0 million, corresponding to the 0.7 million *White Kerry* votes invalidated in Switching Step A of Part II above.

THE ANATOMY OF THE SWITCHING OPERATION

I. THE COMPOSITE 2000 EXIT POLLS, IN MILLIONS (M)

VOTER CATEGORY	% OF VOTERS	GORE (M)	BUSH (M)	GORE %	BUSH %	GORE+ BUSH (M)	%	NADER & (M)	%	TOTAL VALID (M)	TOTAL INVAL. (M)	INVAL. %
WHITE	80.2	35.9	46.3	32.3	41.7	82.0	74.1	3.6	3.2	85.6	3.2	2.9
BLACK	11.5	11.2	0.7	10.1	0.7	11.9	10.7	0.3	0.3	12.2	0.7	0.6
HISPANIC	6.2	4.5	2.0	4.0	1.8	6.5	5.8	0.1	0.1	6.6	0.3	0.3
ASIAN	2.1	1.1	0.9	1.0	0.8	2.0	1.8	0.1	0.1	2.1	0.1	0.1
TOTALS	100.0	52.7	49.9	47.4	45.0	102.6	92.4	4.1	3.7	106.5	4.3	3.9

Total number of ballots cast (millions) 102.6 + 4.1 = 106.7 + 4.3 = 111.0
Certified total ballots, U.S. Bureau of Census (millions): 111.0
Total percent of all ballots cast (92.4 + 3.7 + 3.9) = 100%

Note: The Gore + Bush Asian vote of 2.1 million is 0.1 million higher than the sum of Gore and Bush Asian votes (1.1 + 0.9 = 2.0 million). This means that 0.1 million Invalid Asian votes were added.

II. THE OFFICIAL 2000 VOTE COUNT, IN MILLIONS (M)

VOTER CATEGORY	% OF VOTERS	GORE (M)	BUSH (M)	GORE %	BUSH %	GORE+ BUSH (M)	%	NADER & (M)	%	TOTAL VALID (M)	TOTAL INVAL. (M)	INVAL. %
WHITE	81.2	35.4	46.7	31.9	42.0	82.1	74.0	3.6	3.2	85.8	5.3	4.8
BLACK	10.4	10.0	0.9	9.0	0.8	10.9	9.8	0.1	0.1	11.0	0.1	0.1
HISPANIC	6.2	4.5	2.0	4.0	1.8	6.5	5.8	0.1	0.1	6.6	0.1	0.0
ASIAN	2.1	1.1	0.9	1.0	0.8	2.0	1.8	0.1	0.1	2.1	0.1	0.1
TOTALS	99.9	51.0	50.5	45.9	45.4	101.5	91.4	3.9	3.5	105.4	5.6	5.0
CERT. TOTAL	100.0	51.0	50.5	45.9	45.4	101.5	91.4	4.1	3.7	105.6	5.4	4.86
ERROR	0.1					0.0	0.0	0.2	0.2	0.2	0.2	0.14

Official total ballots (millions): 101.5 + 3.9 + 5.6 = 111.0
Certified total ballots, U.S. Bureau of Census (millions): 111.0

A comparison between Tables I and II reveals that the total number of votes switched in the Invalid category was 2.8 million: *White Invalid* votes increased by 2.1 million from 3.2 to 5.3 million; the *Black Invalid* category was reduced by 0.6 million from 0.7 to 0.1 million, and the *Hispanic Invalid* votes were diminished from 0.1 million to a nominal zero.

III. VOTES SWITCHED BY ALTERING THE 2000 BLACK GORE-BUSH-NADER SPLIT (IN MILLIONS)

	BL. GORE	WH. GORE	BL. BUSH	WH. BUSH	BL. NADER	WH. NADER	HISP. NADER	BL. INVALID	WH. INVALID	HISP. INVALID
EXIT POLLS	11.2	35.9	0.7	46.3	0.3	3.6	0.1	0.7	3.2	0.1
OFFICIAL COUNT	10.0	35.4	0.9	46.7	0.1	3.6	0.1	0.1	5.3	0.0
SWITCH	-1.2	-0.5	+0.2	+0.4	-0.2	0.0	0.0	-0.6	+2.1	-0.1

IV. RESULTS OF THE 2000 VOTE-SWITCHING OPERATION (IN MILLIONS)

	BLACK SWITCHED	WHITE SWITCHED	HISPANIC SWITCHED	NADER & SWITCHED	INVALID SWITCHED
SWITCHED VOTES	-1.8	+1.0;	-0.1	-0.2*	+1.2;-1.0;-0.2 +0.2;+1.0;-0.1

The Tables I and II above trace the following switches:

1. A total of 1.8 million Black votes were switched—1.2 million from Gore to Invalid, and 0.6 million from *Black Invalid* to *White Invalid*;

2. 0.2 million Black votes originally in the Nader & category (see asterisk) were switched to the Invalid category, followed by validation of originally *Invalid Black* votes which were then switched from the Invalid category to the *Bush Black* category.

3. The remaining switching operations were carried out either within the Invalid category or by switching votes out of the Invalid category: 1.0 million from Invalid to White; 0.6 million from *Black Invalid* to *White Invalid*, and then 0.4 million of these from *White Invalid* to *Bush White* and 0.2 million from *Black Invalid* to *Bush Black*.

Note that the first, simpler switching operation could have been performed fairly easily in any voting district. However, the second and third procedures, which are far more complicated, could have been performed only where Republicans enjoy exclusive control of the election machinery under rules and procedures that they themselves had crafted.

V. THE EARLY COMPOSITE 2004 EXIT POLLS, IN MILLIONS (M)

VOTER CATEGORY	% OF TOTAL	KERRY (M)	BUSH (M)	KERRY %	BUSH %	NADER & (M)	NADER &,%	KERRY+ BUSH (M)	%	VALID TOTAL (M)
WHITE	73.58	40.4	53.3	31.4	41.4	1.0	0.77	93.7	72.8	94.7
BLACK	11.66	13.6	1.3	10.6	1.0	0.1	0.08	14.9	11.6	15.0
HISPANIC	7.61	6.6	3.0	5.1	2.3	0.2	0.15	9.6	7.5	9.8
ASIAN	2.00	1.5	1.1	1.2	0.8	0.0	0.00	2.6	2.0	2.6
VALID TOTAL	94.85	62.1	58.7	48.3	45.5	1.3	1.00	120.8	93.9	122.1
INVALIDATED VOTES										6.6
TOTAL										128.7

VI. THE INTERMEDIATE COMPOSITE 2004 EXIT POLLS, IN MILLIONS (M)

VOTER CATEGORY	% OF TOTAL	KERRY (M)	BUSH (M)	KERRY %	BUSH %	NADER & (M)	NADER &,%	KERRY+ BUSH (M)	%	VALID TOTAL (M)
WHITE	73.58	39.7	53.3	30.8	41.4	1.0	0.77	93.0	72.3	94.0
BLACK	11.66	13.6	1.3	10.6	1.0	0.1	0.08	14.9	11.6	15.0
HISPANIC	7.61	6.6	3.0	5.1	2.3	0.2	0.15	9.6	7.5	9.8
ASIAN	2.00	1.5	1.1	1.2	0.8	0.0	0.00	2.6	2.0	2.6
VALID TOTAL	94.85	61.4	58.7	47.7	45.5	1.3	1.00	120.1	93.4	121.4
INVALIDATED VOTES										7.3
TOTAL										128.7

VII. THE LATE COMPOSITE 2004 EXIT POLLS, IN MILLIONS (M)

VOTER CATEGORY	% OF TOTAL	KERRY (M)	BUSH (M)	KERRY %	BUSH %	NADER & (M)	NADER &,%	KERRY+ BUSH (M)	%	VALID TOTAL (M)
WHITE	73.58	39.7	53.3	30.8	41.4	1.0	0.77	93.0	72.3	94.0
BLACK	11.66	13.1	1.8	10.6	1.0	0.1	0.08	14.9	11.6	15.0
HISPANIC	7.61	6.15	3.45	5.1	2.3	0.2	0.15	9.6	7.5	9.8
ASIAN	2.00	1.5	1.1	1.2	0.8	0.0	0.00	2.6	2.0	2.6
VALID										
TOTAL	94.85	60.5	59.6	47.0	46.3	1.3	1.00	120.1	93.4	121.4
INVALIDATED VOTES										7.3
TOTAL										128.7

VIII. THE OFFICIAL 2004 VOTE COUNT, IN MILLIONS (M)

VOTER CATEGORY	% OF TOTAL	KERRY (M)	BUSH (M)	KERRY %	BUSH %	NADER & (M)	NADER &,%	KERRY+ BUSH (M)	%	VALID TOTAL (M)
WHITE	75.21	40.1	55.8	31.2	43.4	0.9	0.70	95.9	74.5	96.8
BLACK	11.42	13.1	1.6	10.2	1.2	0.0	0.00	14.7	11.4	14.7
HISPANIC	6.22	4.3	3.5	3.3	2.7	0.2	0.15	7.8	6.1	8.0
ASIAN	2.00	1.5	1.1	1.2	0.9	0.0	0.00	2.6	2.0	2.6
VALID										
TOTAL	94.85	59.0	62.0	45.9	48.2	1.1	0.85	121.0	94.0	122.1
INVALIDATED VOTES										6.6

The possibility that Bush increased his 31 percent share of the Hispanic vote in 2000 by 12 percentage points to 43 percent in 2004 is vanishingly small. Moreover, the predominantly Catholic and significantly nonwhite Hispanic constituency is not attracted to an Anglo-Saxon, fundamentalist-Protestant, right-wing candidate from Texas like Bush. By contrast, Kerry is a Catholic whose economic program is far more attractive to the Hispanic community than Bush's.

IX. OFFICIAL 2000–2004 PRO-BUSH SWITCH OF HISPANIC VOTES

STATE	TOTAL VOTE (M)	HISP. VOTE %	HISP. (M)	% BUSH E.P. %	% BUSH OFF. %	% KERRY E.P. %	% KERRY OFF. %	BUSH SWITCH ADVANTAGE %	BUSH SWITCH ADVANTAGE (M)
ARIZ.	1.6	12	0.19	31	43	68	56	12	0.046
CALIF.	9.8	21	2.05	35	39	63	59	4	0.164
FLA.	7.3	15	1.10	44	56	56	44	12	0.264
COLO.	1.9	8	0.15	26	30	72	68	4	0.006
GA.	3.2	4	0.12	43	56	68	55	13	0.030
N. MEX.	0.7	32	0.22	32	44	66	54	12	0.054
N.J.	3.4	10	0.34	35	43	63	55	8	0.054
N.Y.	6.8	9	0.60	18	24	74	68	6	0.072
TEX.	7.3	20	1.46	43	49	56	50	6	0.174
TOTAL	42.0	14 (AVG)	6.23						0.864

X. OFFICIAL 2000–2004 PRO-BUSH SWITCH OF BLACK VOTES

STATE	TOTAL VOTE (M)	BLK. VOTE %	BLK. (M)	%BUSH E.P. %	%BUSH OFF. %	%KERRY E.P. %	%KERRY OFF. %	BUSH SWITCH ADVANTAGE %	BUSH SWITCH ADVANTAGE (M)
CALIF.	9.8	6	0.59	11	18	88	81	7	0.08
FLA.	7.3	12	0.88	7	13	92	86	6	0.11
GA.	3.2	25	0.80	7	12	92	87	5	0.08
LA.	1.9	27	0.51	6	9	93	90	3	0.03
MICH.	4.8	13	0.62	8	10	91	89	2	0.02
MISS.	1.1	34	0.37	3	10	96	89	7	0.05
N.C.	3.4	26	0.88	9	14	90	85	5	0.09
N.J.	3.4	14	0.48	35	17	63	55	6	0.06
N.Y.	6.8	13	0.88	8	9	91	90	1	0.02
OHIO	5.5	10	0.55	9	16	90	83	7	0.08
PENN.	5.6	13	0.73	7	16	92	83	9	0.13
S.C.	1.5	30	0.45	7	15	92	84	8	0.07
TENN.	2.4	13	0.31	8	9	91	90	1	0.01
TEX.	7.3	20	1.46	43	49	56	50	6	0.17
TOTAL	64.0	18.3 (AVG)	9.51						1.00

The total advantage Bush received via the switching of Hispanic and Black votes (0.864 million + 1.00 million = 1.86 million) closely matches the 1.9 million fraud calculated at the end of paragraph B on page 191.

XI. INTERIOR CHANGES PRODUCED BY THE 2000 VOTE-SWITCHING OPERATION (IN MILLIONS)

VOTE CATEGORY	INCREASE	DECREASE	FROM	TO	
WHITE GORE	0.0	0.4	35.8	35.4	
BLACK GORE	0.0	1.2	11.2	10.0	
HISPANIC GORE	0.0	0.0	4.5	4.5	
ASIAN GORE	0.0	0.0	1.1	1.1	
INVALID GORE	2.1	0.0	1.5	3.6	
WHITE BUSH	0.5	0.0	46.2	46.7	
BLACK BUSH	0.2	0.0	0.7	0.9	
HISPANIC BUSH	0.0	0.0	2.0	2.0	
ASIAN BUSH	0.0	0.0	0.9	0.9	
INVALID BUSH	0.0	1.0	2.8	1.8	
WHITE NADER &	0.0	0.0	3.6	3.6	
BLACK NADER &	0.0	0.3	0.3	0.0	
HISPANIC NADER &	0.1	0.1	0.2	0.1	
ASIAN NADER &	0.0	0.0	0.1	0.1	
INVALID NADER &	0.0	0.2	0.2	0.0	
TOTALS	2.9	3.1	111.0	111.0	
CERT. TOTAL BALLOTS			111.0	111.0	

XII. 2000 DISTRIBUTION OF INVALID VOTES, IN MILLIONS (M)

VOTE CATEG.	GORE EST.	GORE OFF.	BUSH EST.	BUSH OFF.	NADER EST.	NADER OFF.	GORE DIFF.	BUSH DIFF.	NADER DIFF.	TOTAL DIFF.
WHITE	0.7	3.5	2.4	1.8	0.1	0.0	+2.8	-0.6	-0.1	+2.1
BLACK	0.6	0.0	0.1	0.0	0.0	0.0	-0.6	-0.1	0.0	-0.7
HISPANIC	0.1	0.0	0.1	0.0	0.1	0.0	-0.1	-0.1	-0.1	-0.3
ASIAN	0.1	0.1	0.0	0.0	0.0	0.0	0.0	0.0	0.0	0.0
TOTAL	1.5	3.6	2.6	1.8	0.2	0.0	+2.1	-0.8	-0.2	+1.1

XIII. INTERIOR CHANGES PRODUCED BY THE 2004 VOTE-SWITCHING OPERATION (IN MILLIONS)

VOTE CATEGORY	INCREASE	DECREASE	FROM	TO
WHITE KERRY	0.0	0.3	40.4	40.1
BLACK KERRY	0.0	0.5	13.6	13.1
HISPANIC KERRY	0.0	2.3	6.6	4.3
ASIAN KERRY	0.0	0.0	1.5	1.5
INVALID KERRY	0.2	0.0	3.4	3.6
WHITE BUSH	2.5	0.0	53.3	55.8
BLACK BUSH	0.3	0.0	1.3	1.6
HISPANIC BUSH	0.5	0.0	3.0	3.5
ASIAN BUSH	0.0	0.0	1.1	1.1
INVALID BUSH	0.0	0.2	3.2	3.0
WHITE NADER &	0.0	0.0	1.1	1.1
BLACK NADER &	0.0	0.1	0.1	0.0
HISPANIC NADER &	0.0	0.1	0.2	0.1
ASIAN NADER &	0.0	0.0	0.0	0.0
INVALID NADER &	0.0	0.0	0.0	0.0
TOTALS	3.5	3.5	128.7	128.7
CERT. TOTAL BALLOTS			128.7	128.7

XIV. 2004 DISTRIBUTION OF INVALID VOTES, IN MILLIONS (M)

VOTE CATEG.	KERRY EST.	KERRY OFF.	BUSH EST.	BUSH OFF.	NADER EST.	NADER OFF.	KERRY DIFF.	BUSH DIFF.	NADER DIFF.	TOTAL DIFF.
WHITE	2.4	4.4	2.8	0.8	0.0	0.0	+2.0	-2.0	0.0	0.0
BLACK	0.8	0.8	0.1	0.0	0.0	0.0	0.0	-0.1	0.0	0.0
HISPANIC	0.3	0.2	0.2	0.2	0.0	0.0	0.0	0.0	0.0	0.0
ASIAN	0.0	0.1	0.0	0.0	0.0	0.0	+0.1	0.0	0.0	0.0
TOTAL	3.5	5.5	3.1	1.0	0.0	0.0	+2.1	-2.1	-0.0	0.0

■   ■   ■

I do not believe that CNN, the *New York Times* and all the other major media institutions were unaware of these gross inconsistencies in the 2000 and 2004 election returns. For example, the *New York Times* published two election summaries on November 4 and 7, 2004 which differed significantly in the statistical data presented. Yet it cited the official result without comment, even though the data in its summaries yielded results that differed significantly from the official figures.

The CNN cable network broadcast a continuous stream of election results well in the day following the 2004 election. These reports bristled with striking changes and contradictions. Raw exit-poll and vote-count data broadcasts between 8 pm on election day and noon the following day varied from an initial Kerry lead of 3.4 million votes through successively dwindling Kerry leads of 3.0, 2.5, 1.5, 0.5 million votes through the late night, to a dead heat (60.5 million to 60.5 million) the following morning.

By the time the evening news broadcasts reported a "decisive" Bush victory by exactly 3 million votes, CNN had reported changing Bush leads of 1.0, 1.5, 2.0, 2.5, 3.0, 4.0, and finally 3.0 million votes. I leave it to mathematicians to calculate the vanishingly small possibility that this combined set of facts could exist without some controlling pattern as their source. It is certain any connection of these damning dots would severely tax the credulity of any thinking person.

Consequently, it would seem reasonable to conclude that the mainstream media, in direct violation of its primary mission and its institutional code of ethics, has consciously decided to do all in its power as an institution to prevent the public from connecting the dots. Not only has this hallowed "Free Press" decided not to speak truth to power; it has embarked on a crusade to prevent others from doing so. Not only is it failing to connect the dots, it is feverishly trying to hide them and, when possible, to erase them.

I can find no other explanation for the behavior of the *New York Times* in the aftermath of the 2000 and 2004 elections.

On November 7 and 10, 2000, respectively, the *New York Times* published two differing summaries of the data underlying the final vote count in the presidential election. Both summaries claimed to substantiate the official result: Gore 51.0 million, Bush 50.0 million. However, certain critical numbers in the summaries (see the highlighted section directly below) differed significantly. I used the data in the summaries to calculate my own estimates of the results that derive from the *Times*'s data:

ESTIMATE OF THE 2000 ELECTION, IN MILLIONS
(FROM THE *NEW YORK TIMES*, NOVEMBER 7, 2000)

GROUP	GORE	BUSH	VALID %TOTAL	%DEM	%REP	NADER &
WHITE	35.9	46.3	77.0	42.0	54.0	3.6
BLACK	11.2	0.7	11.0	92.0	6.0	0.3
HISPANIC	4.5	2.0	6.0	67.0	31.0	0.1
ASIAN	1.1	0.9	2.0	54.0	41.0	0.1
SUBTOTAL	52.7	49.9	96.0			4.1
	[47.5%]	[44.9%]	[92.4%]			[3.7%]

Valid votes for Gore plus Bush = 102.6 million = 92.4%
Valid votes for Nader, et al. = 4.1 million = 3.7%
Total valid votes = 106.7 million = 96.1%
Total invalid ballots = 4.3 million = 3.9%
Total ballots = 111.0 million = 100.0%
Certified total ballots = 111.0 million = 100.0%
Error = 0.1 million = 0.1%

ESTIMATE OF THE 2000 ELECTION, IN MILLIONS
(FROM THE *NEW YORK TIMES*, NOVEMBER 10, 2000)

GROUP	GORE	BUSH	VALID %TOTAL	%DEM	%REP	NADER &
WHITE	35.4	46.7	78.0	42.0	54.0	3.43
BLACK	10.0	0.9	10.0	90.0	8.0	0.22
HISPANIC	4.5	2.0	6.0	67.0	31.0	0.13
ASIAN	1.1	0.9	2.0	54.0	41.0	0.11
SUBTOTAL	51.0	50.5	96.0			3.89
	[45.9%]	[45.5%]	[91.4%]			[3.7%]

Valid votes for Gore plus Bush = 101.5 million = 91.4%
Valid votes for Nader, et al. = 3.9 million = 3.7%
Total valid votes = 105.4 million = 95.1%
Total invalid ballots = 5.6 million = 4.9%
Total ballots = 111.0 million = 100.0%

Clearly, the different data in the two different summaries produces radically different results. The 2.8 Kerry win reflected in the early exit polls is duly reflected by the *Times*'s initial summary published on November 7, 2000. When the *Times* published different data four days later, no mention was made of the fact that the changes had produced a whop-

ping 2.3-million-vote change in the election result. (Note the highlights underscoring th
effect of the data changes on the Gore and Bush votes.)

ESTIMATE OF THE 2004 ELECTION, IN MILLIONS
(FROM THE *NEW YORK TIMES*, NOVEMBER 4, 2004)

GROUP	KERRY	BUSH	VALID %TOTAL	%DEM	%REP
WHITE	39.5	54.5	77.0	41.0	58.0
BLACK	11.8	1.5	11.0	88.0	11.0
HISPANIC	5.5	4.3	8.0	56.0	43.0
ASIAN	1.4	1.1	2.0	56.0	44.0
SUBTOTAL	58.2	61.4	98.0		
	[48.7%]	[50.3%]	[99.0%]		

Votes for Kerry plus Bush = 119.6 million = 92.9
Votes for Nader, et al. = 1.3 million = 1.0
Total valid votes = 120.9 million = 93.9
Invalidated ballots = 7.8 million = 6.1
Overall total votes = 128.7 million = 100.0

ESTIMATE OF THE 2004 ELECTION, IN MILLIONS
(FROM THE *NEW YORK TIMES*, NOVEMBER 7, 2004)

GROUP	KERRY	BUSH	VALID %TOTAL	%DEM	%REP
WHITE	39.6	55.9	79.0	39.0	55.0
BLACK	13.6	1.7	12.0	88.0	11.0
HISPANIC	4.3	3.3	6.0	56.0	43.0
ASIAN	1.5	1.1	2.0	58.0	44.0
SUBTOTAL	59.0	62.0	99.0		
	[48.0%]	[51.0%]			

Votes for Kerry plus Bush = 121.0 million = 94.0
Votes for Nader, et al. = 1.1 million = 0.9
Total valid votes = 122.1 million = 94.9
Invalidated ballots = 6.6 million = 5.1
Overall total votes = 128.7 million = 100.0

The highlighted figures in the two summaries underscore the effect of the data change
on the numbers of votes credited to Kerry and Bush. However, this time the vote spread
between the candidates are almost identical. Moreover, the 0.2 million difference (3.

million vs. 3.0 million) matches the 0.2 million difference between the Nader votes (1.3 million vs. 1.1 million). The difference in the vote spreads of the Hispanic Kerry-Bush split: (5.5–4.3) vs. (4.3–3.3) amounts to 1.2 million–1.0 million or 0.2 million which accounts for the 0.2 million advantage Bush received from the "lost" Nader votes.

Note that the Black percentage of the total vote is reported as 11 percent in the first summary and 12 percent in the second summary—a discrepancy of 1 percent amounting to 1.3 million votes. Moreover, the missing 1 percent of the vote in the first summary (the total Valid vote adds up to only 98 percent of the total Valid vote instead of 99 percent) indicates the fraudulent disappearance or illegal suppression of at least that number of Black votes. The difference between the Kerry-Bush splits of the Black vote: (11.8–1.5) vs. (13.6–1.7) amounts to the difference between Kerry advantages of 10.3 percent and 11.9 million, or 1.6 million votes. If this number is added to Kerry's total cited in the November 4 *Times* summary, Bush's lead is cut in half: Kerry 59.8 million–Bush 61.4 million.

■ ■ ■

The following questions must be asked: Did the *New York Times* and the other major media institutions knowingly cover up the greatest vote fraud in modern history? Moreover, why have all these institutions, including the *Times*, refused to release to the public any of the raw data upon which their exit polls and election analyses were based?

The *Times*'s public editor is duty bound to pursue this issue relentlessly. In any case, the American people are duty bound to demand answers on this matter from the President and Vice President of the United States.

INDEX

abolitionist movement, 114
affirmative action
    Black middle class benefited by, 71–72
    redefining, 87
    workplace discrimination combated by,
        73–74
Afghanistan war
    regime change purpose of, 55–56
    U.S. failure of, 64
AFL. *See* American Federation of Labor
AFL-CIO, 94–95
African Americans. *See also* Black Americans;
    Blacks; Negroes
    as dual national self-identification, 3
    political energy of, 154
    slave labor reparations for, 81n1
    unquenchable spirits of, 162
    voters illegally disfranchised, 192
    whites accepting, 4
Against All Enemies (Clarke), 27
America, 166
American Dream, 8
American Federation of Labor (AFL), 94
Americans
    America's image cherished by white, 41
    cultural traits shared by, 30
    economic depression for, 117
    political system cleaned up by, 112
    promised revolution fulfilled for, 182
    religious growth for, 182
    WASP gave way to, 18
ancestry, 3
Anglo-Saxon Protestant culture
    Bush, George W., constituency made up
        of, 28
    Founding Fathers as, 8
    immigrants assimilated into, 4, 5
    race issue used by, 14–15
armed forces
    Blacks disproportionate in, 165
    ghetto pacification by, 132
    Negroes treated equally in, 164
    universal draft for, 77
Ashcroft, John, 41
assassination
    Johnson, Andrew, president from, 32–33
    Kennedy, John F., 158–59

    King, 131
    Lincoln, 116–17
    Malcolm X, 131, 158–59
    right-wing faction performing, 127–28
Association of Federal, State, County and
    Municipal Employees (AFSCME), 76
atom-bomb, 119
Atta, Mohammad, 60–61
AWOL, 48

Berlin Wall, 141
Black(s)
    in armed forces, 165
    Bush, George W., administration not
        trusted by, 27
    Bush, George W., administration paying
        off, 85
    civil rights leadership credibility lost for,
        168
    civil rights movement bypassing, 131–32
    conservatives not supported by, 13
    education funding for, 91
    ethical guidelines of, 16
    fraudulently switching votes of, 102, 105
    historical icons for, 162–63
    invalid votes for, 112n1
    Jackson, Jesse, galvanizing, 138
    as Judeo-Christians, 17
    Kennedy, John F., tribute from, 160–61
    mass media corrupting, 180–81
    minority issue transformed from, 88
    Mondale chosen by, 138
    political power of, 153
    progressive interests shared with, 156
    Progressive Party supported by, 121
    Progressive Party supporting, 154–55
    Republican Party enemy to, 43, 96–97
    rights abolished for, 117
    self-identification as, 5
    significant gains for, 113
    slave population percentage for, 10
    spiritual faith for, 16
    switching operations victimizing, 102, 105,
        197, 200
    voting power growing for, 145, 180
Black Americans. *See also* African Americans;
    Blacks

Bush, George W., policies/culture
  opposed by, 52, 53
Bush, George W., policies hurting, 75
civil rights claimed by, 148n3
class interests of, 86
congress without Republican, 31
Constitution faith from, 8
demands for, 154–55
Democratic advantage from, 167
economic interests assaulted for, 78
equal opportunity lacking for, 89–90
firefighter induction lacking, 23
as freedom people, 12
historical icons for, 162–63
New Deal economy favored by, 69
9/11 policy skepticism by, 27
oppression of, 125
political solidarity of, 167
poverty rates of, 79
progressive agenda supported by, 13
public sector employing, 76
repressive years for, 115
Republican Party abandoned by, 118
right-wing enemies of, 51
self-identification as, 1–2
small business ownership for, 80
state terror experienced by, 26
teacher recruiting of, 92
trade union focus for, 97
unemployment rates double for, 75–76
Union Army with, 116
Black Caucus, 110
Black community
  conflicts exposed for, 20
  rioting in, 132
Black culture
  day's work valued by, 69–70
  Thomas rejecting, 37
  universe seen by, 184n4
Black freedom movement, 74
Black ghetto masses, 161–62
Black institutions, 5
Black-labor progressive base, 143
Black leaders, 124
  bankruptcy of, 84–85
  credibility lost in civil rights movement
    by, 168
  Democratic Party benefiting from, 145
Black middle class
  affirmative action benefiting, 71–72
  leadership failing for, 83–84
  mass media obsessed by, 180–81
  right wing leadership followed by, 70–71
  significant gains for, 7–8
Black-nationalist ideology, 160
Black Panthers—Oakland, 7
Black power, 180

Black Power movement
  minority following, 71
  radical wing forming, 157–58
  working class leading, 7
Blackwell, J. Kenneth, 105
Black working class
  armed forces opportunities for, 77
  Black Power movement led by, 7
  civil rights movement by, 123–24
  discontent of, 158
  economic interests of, 88
  economic justice sought by, 118
  NAACP endowment unrelated to, 91
  old culture traditions of, 70
  priority given to, 87
  Progressive Party supported by, 121
Bond, Julian, 93
Boxer, Barbara, 110–11
Brezhnev, Leonid, 147n2
budget cuts, 78
Bush administration (George W.)
  Black leadership payoffs from, 85
  Blacks skeptical about, 27
  Confederacy legacy and, 28–29
  Daeubler-Gmelin criticizing, 59
  deficits from, 77–78
  federal workforce downsized by, 76
  foreign policy detrimental from, 50, 56
  Iraqi revenue-producing abilities sought
    by, 62
  Iraqi withdrawal plan of, 63
  legal foundation established for, 75
  military establishment contradicting, 66
  9/11 terrorist attack cover-up by, 55
  totalitarian traditions from, 28
  unscrupulous, 107
  victim's trust lost for, 47–48
  white mass media covering, 29
Bush, George H. W.
  fifth Confederate coup during term of, 37
  Gorbachev challenged by, 141–42
  Gorbachev warning, 143–44
  Perot dooming reelection of, 144
  Yeltsin deal with, 150n10
Bush, George W. *See also* Bush Administration
    (George W.)
  "bad pilot" remark from, 47
  Black's economic situation worsened by,
    75
  Black's opposing, 52–53
  character flaws of, 50–51
  Confederate coup by, 31–32, 40–41
  constituency of, 28
  Gore's votes stolen by, 102–3
  Hispanic votes and, 199
  imperial presidency by, 42
  inadequate resume of, 48–49

lying about Iraq, 64
New South Confederacy from, 31–32
no action from, 45–46
preemptive war policy of, 53–54
presidential election 2000 votes for,
    187–89
presidential election 2004 votes for,
    189–90
as religious zealot, 41
removal of, 183
Roosevelt, Theodore, hero of, 57
ultraconservative control gained from,
    168
United Nations alienated by, 60
votes gained by, 200
war disastrous for, 63
war speech from, 65

campaign, 142
Carter, Jimmy, 134
Casey, George W., 66
caste system, 15
Cayuhoga County, 109
census (1790), 115
Change to Win Coalition, 95
character flaws, 50–51
cheat sheets, 109
China, 122
Christian, born-again, 137
Christian Nation, 42
CIO. *See* Congress of Industrial Organiza-
    tion
citizenship, 9–10
civic principles, 14–15
Civil Rights Acts of 1965
    de facto segregation not outlawed by, 86
    flaw residing in, 73
    Johnson, Lyndon B., signing, 70
    legal segregation ended by, 7
civil rights movement
    Black Americans claiming, 148n3
    black leadership credibility lost in, 168
    Blacks bypassed by, 131–32
    black working class assisting, 123–24
    economic justice from, 80–81
    equal legal rights from, 6
    federally enforced, 33
    as irresistible wave, 126
    King leading, 124
    mission important for, 92–93
    political basis for, 90–91
    radical wing of, 157–58
Civil War, 115
Clarke, Richard, 27
class priorities
    human priorities transcending, 140
    race overtaken by, 83

class war, 84
Clinton, Bill
    economic slide halted by, 74
    Helms threatening life of, 39–40
    impeachment attempt against, 40
    right-wing conspiracy stated by, 39
    vote statistics for, 144–45
Clinton-Gore Democratic ticket, 145
Clinton, Hillary, 175
coalition forces, 62
Coalition of Black Trade Unionists, 95
Cold War
    atom-bomb launching, 119
    demilitarization ending, 147n2
    Gorbachev ending, 120, 152n10
    Reagan and, 139
collective memory, 162
collective well-being, 70
color-blind, 6
colored people, 6
color prejudice, 6
command post, 23
communications, 22–23
Communist movement
    Engels cofounder of, 11–12
    Marx cofounder of, 11–12
Communist Party
    power undermined in, 139
    Progressive Party branded, 121–22
    Truman fighting, 122
community, 14
Confederate coup
    Bush, George H. W., and, 37
    Bush, George W., election hijacking as,
        40–41
    Clinton impeachment attempt as, 40
    Kennedy, John F., victim of, 33–34
    Lincoln assassinated by, 32
    Republican Party perpetrating, 31
    Supreme Court subverted by, 38
    Watergate as, 36
Confederate values
    Bush administration building on, 28–29
    Bush, George W., establishing, 31–32
    Reagan confirming, 36–37
Congress, 31
Congress of Industrial Organization (CIO),
    94, 113, 118
Conservative America, 12–13
conservatives. *See also* ultraconservatives
    black voters not supporting, 13
    ideological challenge to, 35
    racist tendencies for, 155–56
    ultraconservatives and, 130
conspiracy
    Eisenhower warning of, 38–39
    Helms leading, 39–40

leadership invisible for, 37
  theory of, 148n5
Constitution, U.S.
  amendments to, 9
  Black American's faith in, 8
  original intent for, 185n10
Conyers, John, 107
corporations, 174
Cosby, Bill, 85
coup, 151n10
crimes, 107–8
Cuban missile crisis, 147n2
cultural assimilation, 18, 19
cultural traditions
  equality sought for, 20
  slaves with, 5
culture, 29–30, 181
cynicism, 25–26

Daeubler-Gmelin, Herta, 59
Dallek, Robert, 128–29
Davis, Ossie, 159
Dean, Howard, 175
Declaration of Independence, 114
  language of, 10
  population at time of, 9
defense strategy document, 53
DeLay, Tom, 40
demilitarization, 140, 147n2
democracy, 99
Democratic Party
  Black Americans benefiting, 167
  Black-labor progressive base for, 143
  Blacks deliver advantage to, 153
  Blacks present increasing votes for, 145
  Black voters for, 96, 184n1
  as center party, 170
  Hispanic votes for, 106
  leaders betrayal of, 111
  leaders elimination influencing, 133
  as liberals/progressives, 155
  lower income focus for, 173–74
  opposition party shunned by, 169
  political army for, 169
  Progressive Party and, 176
  as sharply divided, 175
Department of Defense, 29
deregulation, 76, 136–37
Detroit riot, 132
discrimination, 72–73
  affirmative action combating, 73–74
  equal treatment clause for, 88
  federally enforced quotas for, 89
  quotas and, 87–88
  supply-side economics intensifying, 83–84
diversity, 38
divine wisdom, 179

DuBois, W.E.B., 83
Dukakis, Michael, 142–43

economic depression, 117
economic issues
  King pursuing, 80–81
  political challenges for, 84
  supply-side, 83–84
economic justice, 118
economic policy, 74, 90
economic program, 172, 199
economy, 36
education, 91
Edwards, John
  landslide victory projected for, 180
  as president, 175
  progressive caucus committed to, 176
Eisenhower, Dwight D.
  conspiracy warning from, 38–39
  election of, 122–23
  preemptive war not considered by, 58–59
election officials
  Republican controlled, 192
  voter lists purged by, 108
election results, 100–101
electoral college system
  democracy requiring, 99
  election fraud possible from, 100
employers, 72–73
Engels, Friedrich, 11–12
equal opportunity
  armed forces providing, 164
  Blacks lacking, 89–90
  campaign for, 86–89
  Kennedy, John F., committed to, 34
  King focus shifted to, 85–86
Ervin, Sam, 27, 35, 149n7
ethnic groups, 1
exit polls
  composite of (2000), 195
  composite of (2004), 198
  Gore victory predicted by, 101
  Kerry winning in, 110
  official results different from, 99–100
  vote percentages from, 103–4
exit strategy, 63, 172

fair trade, 174, 177
faith-based initiative, 105
fascism, 137
Federal Aviation Authority, 47
Federal Bureau of Investigation (FBI)
  flight schools visited by, 46
  liberties trampled by, 120
federal workforce, 76
Fields, C. Virginia, 21–22
Fifth Amendment, 114

firefighters
    all-white ceremony inducting, 23, 30n2
    communications lost to, 23
    perished unnecessarily, 22
fiscal conservative, 179
flight school, 46
Ford, Gerald, 134
foreign policy
    Bush administration's detrimental, 50, 56
    Eisenhower's, 123
    Johnson, Lyndon, reversing, 126
    militaristic, 53
    Progressive Parties, 177
    Reagan's, 139
    ultraconservative obsolete as, 141
    War Against Terror used in, 54
Founding Fathers, 8
"Four Freedoms," 12
Fourteenth Amendment, 88, 106, 154, 174
freedom, 10–11
free trade agreements, 75, 76
Frist, Bill, 40

genocide, 82n1, 166
German Justice Minister, 59
ghetto masses. *See also* Black ghetto masses
    growing power of, 180
    mass media corrupting, 181
    oppressors message from, 161
    volunteer military for, 164
ghetto pacification, 132
Giuliani, Rudy
    communities racially polarized by, 21
    "Great White Father" as, 24
    leadership test failed by, 22
globalization, 54–55, 75
Gorbachev, Mikhail
    Bush, H. W., challenge for, 141–42
    Bush, H. W., warnings from, 143–44
    Cold War ended by, 120, 152n10
    demilitarization by, 140
    Soviet Union dissolution by, 139
    Yazov coup leader against, 150n10
Gordon, Bruce S., 90
Gore, Al, 101
    Bush stealing votes from, 102–3
    Clinton Democratic ticket for, 145
    exit poll victory prediction for, 101
    presidential election 2000 votes for,
        187–89
government, 168
Grant, Ulysses S., 117
"Great White Father," 24
Gulf war. *See* Iraq war

Haig, Alexander, 149n7
Hauser, Philip M., 166

Havel, Vaclav, 60–61
health care, 174
Helms, Jesse, 39–40
Hill, Eleanor, 43, 46
Hispanic votes
    Bush, George W., and, 199
    Democratic Party abandonment unlikely
        for, 106
    invalidated, 191
Hitler, Adolf, 28
Hoover, J. Edgar, 120
human priorities, 140
human race, 14–15
human rights, 154–55, 172
human self-identification, 160
Humphrey, Hubert, 133
Hussein, Saddam, 56

immigrants, 4, 5
impeachment, 32, 40
imperial presidency, 42
independent commission, 46
industrial economy, 118–19
Inouye, Daniel, 37
international treaties, 50
invalid category. *See* switching operations; votes
investigation (9/11), 46–48
Iran, 135–36
Iran-contra scandal, 36–37
Irangate, 136
Iraq
    aid for, 61–62
    Bush, George W., withdrawal from, 63
    civilian casualties in, 63–64
    occupation of, 60–61
    reconstruction of, 82n2
Iraq war
    Bush, George W., lying about, 64
    illegal, 56
    opposition to, 172
    Powell recommending end to, 143
Iroquois Confederation, 11
Islamic extremism
    political exploitation by, 65
    U.S. foreign policy causing, 56
Italian intelligence, 45

Jackson, Jesse, 96
    Blacks galvanized by, 138
    presidential run by, 142
Jefferson, Thomas, 116
Jesus of Nazareth, 16
"JFK's Second Term" (Dallek), 128–29
Johnson, Andrew
    assassination cleared way for, 32–33
    counterrevolution led by, 117
    impeachment escaped by, 32

Johnson, Lyndon B.
  Civil Rights Act signed by, 70
  Kennedy, John F., succeeded by, 35
  policy reversal by, 126
  War on Poverty institutionalized by, 133
Judeo-Christians, 17

Keane, Thomas, 43
Kennedy, Anthony, 74
Kennedy, John F.
  assassination of, 158–59
  Black tribute to, 160–61
  equal opportunity commitment from, 34,
    52n1
  foreign policy reversed for, 126
  inaugural address by, 124–25
  Johnson, Lyndon B., succeeding, 35
  New Deal invoked by, 34–35
  progressive agenda by, 130–31
  right-wing faction targeted by, 128–29
  second coup against, 33–34
  as unique president, 128
Kerry, John
  economic program more attractive by, 199
  exit polls for, 110
  presidential election 2004 votes for,
    189–90
Khomeini, Ayatollah Ruhollah, 135
Khrushchev, Nikita, 123, 125
  Brezhnev succeeding, 147n
  Strangelove superbombs ordered by,
    148n6
King, Martin Luther
  assassination of, 131
  civil rights movement led by, 124
  economic issues from, 80–81
  equal opportunity focus from, 85–86
  historical address by, 157
  "meek shall inherit . . . earth" from, 183
  nonviolent mass action promoted by, 70
  Poor People's March led by, 7
King of Harlem, 160
Ku Klux Klan, 120, 137

labels, 1
labor issues, 72
Latinos, 18–19
Lay, Ken, 49
leadership, 22, 37
  Blacks lacking, 84–85, 124, 145, 168
  Giuliani failing, 22
  presidential, 43
  right wing, 70–71
Lemnitzer, Lyman, 129
liberal-conservative coalition, 125–26
liberal-progressive government, 145
liberals, 131

liberty, 10–11
Lincoln, Abraham
  assassination of, 116–17
  Confederate coup assassinating, 32
  freedom/liberty clarified by, 10–11
  reconstruction policy of, 116
  second American revolution from, 115
Lott, Trent, 40
low income voters, 173–74
Lucy, William, 95

Malcolm X
  assassination of, 131, 158–59
  insightful comments from, 159–60
  slaves referred to by, 3
Mandela, Nelson, 50
Marshall, Thurgood, 38
Marx, Karl, 11–12
mass media
  Black middle class obsessing, 180–81
  conspiracy of silence by, 11
  dissident opinions from, 29
  ghetto masses corrupted by, 181
  journalistic responsibilities abdicated by,
    107
  9/11 obsession created by, 27
  presidential election (2000) cover up by,
    104
  Republican Party conspiring with, 110
  silence of, 136
  voter fraud silence from, 109–10, 203
  white viewpoints offered by, 26
mass media, white
  Bush administration policy denial from,
    29
  political hostility conveyed by, 52
mass movements
  political upheavals with, 170
  Progressive Party created by, 171
  social/political, 79–80
McCarthy, Joseph, 122
McKinley, William, 57
Meredith, James, 34
middle income voters, 184n9
military coup, 149n7
military establishment, 66
Miller, Mark Crispin, 107
minorities, 88
  Black Power movement followed by, 71
  equal opportunity for, 87
  pitted against each other, 19
Mondale, Walter, 138
Moynihan, Daniel, 163
  Negro lower class memo from, 165–66
  volunteer military recommended by, 164
Mueller, Robert, 44
Myers, Richard B., 66

NAACP. *See* National Association for the Advancement of Colored People

Nader, Ralph
black votes disappear for, 191
invalid votes of, 202
vote falsely reduced for, 188
votes for, 187–88
white votes invalidated for, 192

National Association for the Advancement of Colored People (NAACP)
Black working class interests and, 91
Gordon president of, 90
mission missing for, 92–93
outdated name of, 6
as political lobbying group, 93

national security, 49

National Urban League (NUL), 97

Native Americans
death chosen by, 12
genocide of, 82n1
human status denied for, 10
political traditions from, 11

Negroes
armed forces equal treatment for, 164
colored replaced by, 6

The Negro Family (Moynihan), 163

neocons, 130

New Deal
Black Americans favoring, 69
economic program based on, 172
fascism basis for, 137
implementing updated, 155
Kennedy, John F., invoking, 34–35
Progressive Party based on, 175
Roosevelt, Franklin D., winning election with, 117
union-friendly, 95

New York Times
different mood expressed by, 24–25
photo published by, 30n2

9/11 terrorist attacks
Black skepticism toward, policy, 27
Bush, George W., cover-up of, 55
investigation of, 46–48
North Tower evacuated during, 23
presidential leadership preventing, 43
preventing, 45
Republican Party exploiting, 24
warnings ignored for, 27

9/11 victims
investigation launched by, 46–48
speculation by, 48

Nixon administration, 149n7

Nixon, Richard
fascist tendencies of, 35
Humphrey losing to, 133

Moynihan memo to, 165–66
Southern strategy of, 7

Nobel Peace Prize, 152n10

nonvoters
potential political army of, 169
Progressive Party focusing on, 171

North, Oliver, 36–37

NUL. *See* National Urban League

Obama, Barak, 111, 167
progressive caucus committed to, 176
as vice president, 175

O'Connor, Sandra Day, 72, 74, 75

official results, 99–100

Ohio, 104–5

oil industry, 49

opposition party, 112, 169

oppressed people, 125, 162

organized labor, 156

Oswald, Lee Harvey, 33

Paine, Thomas
progressives led by, 114
"Rights of man" by, 116

Perot, Ross, 144

personal growth, 15

personal opportunity, 15

political energy, 154

political landscape, 182

political system
American people cleaning up, 112
black power in, 153
categories of, 155–56
electorate holding, accountable, 170
overthrowing, 146

political traditions, 11

political upheaval, 170

Poor People's March, 7

popular culture, 181

popular slogan, 14

poverty, 79, 157

Powell, Colin, 167
cease fire negotiated by, 144
cease fire recommended by, 143
defense strategy document from, 53
as ideal third-party candidate, 178
landslide victory projected for, 180

preemptive war
Bush, George W., policy of, 53–54
Eisenhower not considering, 58–59

president
imperial, 42
leadership of, 43

presidential election (2000)
Black Caucus challenging, 110
Bush, George W., stealing, 74
Bush, George W., votes in, 187–89

inconsistencies of, 99
media cover-up of, 104
vote fraud in, 187–88
presidential election (2004)
Bush, George W., votes in, 189–94
inconsistencies of, 99
Ohio vote determining, 104–5
Republican conspiracy stealing, 111
vote fraud in, 189–90
white vote advantage in, 184n1
principles, 15
professional middle class, 79–80
progressive agenda
Black Americans supporting, 13
Roosevelt, Franklin D., with, 118–19
Roosevelt/Kennedy with, 130–31
Progressive America, 12–13
progressive caucus, 176
Progressive Party
Black interests supported by, 154–55
Blacks supporting, 121
building process for, 175–76
Communist Party label of, 121–22
creating, 169–70
Democratic Party and, 176
issue-oriented mass movement creating,
171
platform of, 177–78
Wallace leading, 120
progressives
Black interests shared by, 156
Paine leading, 114
ultraconservatives faring no better then,
131
prophets, 182
public sector, 76

Al Qaeda, 45
quotas
court rules, illegal, 72
fixed number from, 73
past discrimination only for, 87–88

race issue
Anglo-Saxon Protestant culture using,
14–15
class overtaking, 83
racial minorities
preferences of, 4
semiassimilation contingent offered to, 19
racial self-identification, 160
racism
conservatives lean towards, 155–56
institutional, 73
Reagan guilty of, 137
Truman ignoring, 120
racist institutional infrastructure, 183

Reagan Revolution, 136–37, 145
Reagan, Ronald
Confederate values confirmed by, 36–37
economy sabotaged by, 36
foreign policy of, 139
Iran negotiating with, 135–36
as openly racist, 137
Russia visited by, 140–41
ultraconservatives launching, 135
Reconstruction policy, 32, 116
religion, 41, 182
Renquist, William, 74
Republican administration
crimes perpetrated by, 107–8
government corrupted by, 168
Republican election officials, 104–5
Republican Party
Black Americans abandoning, 118
Black congressmen lacking for, 31
Blacks abandoned support for, 118
as Black's political enemy, 43, 96–97
campaign dirty by, 142
Confederate coup perpetrated by, 31
as conservatives/ultraconservatives, 155
economic policies of, 90
election officials controlled by, 192
ideological basis of, 170
media collusion with, 110
presidential election stolen by, 111
tragedy exploited by, 24
resignation, 133–34
revolution, 115, 117, 182
Rice, Condoleezza, 59
information known by, 44
personal failure of, 45
right-wing (WASP) conspiracy, 32, 39
right-wing faction
assassination performed by, 127–28
Black Americans enemies to, 51
Black middle class leadership following,
70–71
divine wisdom claimed by, 179
Kennedy, John F., to dismantle, 128–29
right wing leadership, 70–71
Robeson, Paul, 160
Rockefeller, Nelson, 134
Roosevelt, Franklin D.
death of, 119
"Four Freedoms" of, 12
New Deal economy from, 69, 117
New Deal policies from, 155
New Deal update for, 95
poor empowered by, 34
progressive agenda of, 118–19, 130–31
Truman succeeding, 119
two freedoms of, 93–94
Roosevelt, Theodore, 57

Rove, Karl, 57
Rumsfeld, Donald
    briefing continued by, 47
    extremism speech from, 65
Russia, 140–41

Scalia, Antonin, 74
Schlesinger, James, 149n7
Schwartzkopf, Norman, 143
second-class citizenship, 11
Secret Service, 47
segregation, 7, 86
self-identification, 1–3, 5, 160
Shabazz, Attallah, 159
slave labor
    as crime against humanity, 82n1
    reparations for, 81n1
slaves
    African American reparations for being,
        81n1
    Black population percentage of, 10
    caste system rejected by, 15
    census including, 115
    cultural traditions for, 5
    status of, 2–3
    war of Independence fought by, 113–14
small business ownership, 80
social revolution, 146
social security, 174
society, 6
Southern Strategy, 7
Soviet Union
    Gorbachev dissolving, 139
    war results with, 129
spiritual faith, 16
spiritual life, 181
Stalin, Joseph, 119, 123
Starr, Kenneth, 39
state terror, 26
Strangelove superbombs, 148n6
supply-side economics, 83–84
Supreme Court, U.S.
    Confederate coup subverting, 38
    "quotas" illegal from, 72
    vote stealing blessed by, 102–3
Sweeney, John, 94
switching operations
    Blacks victims of, 102, 105
    invalid category used for, 188–91
    Kerry votes canceled for, 189
    2000 vote results from, 197
    vote changes from, 188–94, 197, 200, 201,
        203

Taliban, 55–56
tax cuts, 78
teachers, 92

terrorist attacks
    combating fear of, 26
    wars producing, 55
terrorist reports, 44
"The Rights of Man" (Paine), 116
Thomas, Clarence, 74
    Black culture rejected by, 37
    diversity added by, 38
totalitarian traditions, 28
trade unions, 97
Treasury, 49
Triad computer company, 109
Truman, Harry S
    anti-Communist crusade by, 122
    platform reversed by, 121
    racist repression ignored by, 120
    Roosevelt, Franklin D., succeeded by, 119
two-party system
    political class created by, 130
    swing votes in, 169
    third major party for, 179–80

ultraconservatives
    conservatives and, 130
    control gained for, 168
    foreign policy obsolete, 141
    progressives faring no better then, 131
    Reagan launched by, 135
    Republicans as, 155
unemployment rates, 75–76
Union Army, 116
United Nations
    Bush, George W., alienating, 60
    Iraq control relinquished to, 62–63
United States (U.S.)
    China stand-off with, 122
    globalization program of, 54–55
    Kennedy, John F., unique for, 128
    middle class of, 78–79
    military lead of, 59
    Treasury bankrupted, 49

value system, 14–15
Von Essen, Thomas, 22
Von Hoffman, Nicholas, 51
voters. See also exit polls
    African Americans disfranchised as, 192
    Black power increasing as, 145, 180
    conservatives not supported by, 13
    Democratic Party with Black, 96, 184n1
    lower income, 173
    middle income subgroup of, 184n9
    non, 169, 171
    provisional ballots not received by, 108
votes. See also exit polls
    black invalid decreasing, 112n1
    Black, switched, 197, 200

Bush, George W., gaining, 200
Clinton statistics for, 144–45
exit poll percentages of, 103–4
fraudulent switching of Hispanic, 105, 199
Hispanic, invalidated, 191
illegal alterations to, 189–90
invalidation of, 102, 193, 203
invalid distribution of, 202–3
manipulation of, 100–101, 193–94, 196
Nader invalid, 192, 202
Nader's, 187–88
Nader's black, disappear, 191
official count of (2000), 196
official count of (2004), 199
presidential election advantage from white, 184n1
presidential elections actual, 187
Supreme Court blessing theft of, 102–3
switching operations changing, 188–94, 197, 200, 201, 203
switching operations for, 197, 200
two-party system swing, 169
white, created, 192
white invalid increasing, 112n1, 189
voting fraud, 102–3
Blackwell revealing, 105
Hispanic votes switched for, 199
mass media silent about, 109–10, 203
presidential election with, 187–88, 189–90
voting machines perpetrating, 101
voting machines—electronic
fraud perpetrated on, 101
Republican companies owning, 103
votes transferred by, 109
voting power, 145, 180

Wallace, Henry, 120
War Against Terror
blacks suspicious of, 26
foreign policy acceptance from, 54
War of Independence, 113–14
War on Poverty, 133, 163
Warren Commission, 148n5
Warren County, 109
wars. *See also* Iraq war
Bush, George W., disastrous, 63
terrorist attacks produced by, 55
Washington, Booker T., 84
WASP. *See* White Anglo-Saxon Protestant
Watergate, 36
weapons of mass destruction, 60–61
White Anglo-Saxon Protestant (WASP), 18
agencies dominated by, 52n3
right-wing conspiracy by, 32
white institutions, 5
white majority, 18–19
white votes, 112n1, 192
Williams, Kenneth, 44
Willis, Edwin E., 132
women
discrimination against, 89
second-class citizenship for, 11
World Trade Center, 23

Yazov, Dmitri, 150n10
Yeltsin, Boris
Bush, George H. W., deal with, 150n10
coup warning for, 151n10

tattoos 139
teachers of note, on résumés 134
temping work 19–20
Tenner, Rachel 104
Texas (Austin) 227–31
theatre work
  definition of theatrical casting 95
  in Atlanta 238–42
  in Austin, Texas 230–1
  in Chesapeake Bay area 213, 217–25
  in Chicago 157, 163–5, 166–75
  in Minneapolis/St Paul 176, 178–82
  in New York 190–1
  in Philadelphia 231–2, 234–7
  method for listing credits 132–3
  vs film and TV 201–2
thumbnails 128, 139–40
Tomlin, Lily 125
transport
  driving skills 135
  full fare 76
  in Chesapeake Bay area 213–14
  in Los Angeles 155, 204
  in New York 193
  public transport vs car 77
TV and film work
  auditioning with prepared scenes 150–2
  film and TV casting directors 99–101
  in Austin, Texas 227–31
  in Chicago 156
  in Los Angeles 199–202
  in Minneapolis/St Paul 176
  in New York 192
  in Philadelphia 232
  résumés for 132–3, 135
  vs theatre work 201–3

Twin Cities (Minneapolis and St Paul, Minnesota) 176–89
"type" 111–19

unions
  Actor's Equity Association (AEA) 74, 99, 156, 164
  getting union affiliation before moving to LA/NYC 82, 192, 193–4
  SAG-AFTRA 72–4, 106, 164
  union fees 72–4
  union status on résumés 128
uniqueness, celebrating your 114

vehicles (skills with) 135
video reels 140–1
"Viewpoints" 123–4
voluntary work 28–9, 79

waiting tables 22
Walker, Alyssa 94
wardrobe 75–6, 138, 140, 149–50, 204
Washington DC 213–27
Washington (state) 154
Webb, Spud 112
websites, personal 141
websites, useful
  Austin 228
  Chesapeake Bay Area, DC and Baltimore 214–15, 226
  Chicago 163–5
  Los Angeles 208
  Minneapolis and St Paul, Minnesota 189
  New York 196–7
Whitehead, Dustin 26
Williams Paisley, Kimberley 105
writing your dreams down 12–14

yearly calendars, creating 53–4